THE
NAUTICAL
HOME

*Coastline-Inspired Ideas to Decorate
with Seaside Spirit*

Skyhorse Publishing

Anna Örnberg

Translated by Gun Penhoat

A BIG THANK YOU TO EVERYONE:

Annika Berglund:
whether it's to carry, grind, paint, fix, or
scrape . . . on days when I have Annika
around, the work is both easier and more fun.

Kajsa & Kalle:
my favorite models.

Lena & Bernt:
for a lovely (if blustery) day spent at the great
ship chandler on the Swedish island of Öland.

Agneta /Fronica & Cor/ Malin & Johan:
they opened the doors wide to their lovely
homes for our photography sessions.

Kosta Boda Art Hotel:
their beautiful stone barn became our photography studio for a day.

Thomas:
my supportive and encouraging husband -
year after year, book after book.

Eva:
my editor in Sweden, critic, friend, and brain-
storming partner.

Monica:
she transforms visions into real books.

Marion Beijnink:
photographer and coastal explorer with a
keen eye for poetical beauty.

Tommy:
photographer extraordinaire.

Copyright © 2013 by Anna Örnberg
English Translation © 2015 by Skyhorse
Publishing

First published in 2013 as *Inred med marin
inspiration* by Anna Örnberg, Bokförlaget
Semic, Sundbyberg, Sweden

Photo Tommy Durath

Graphic design Monica Sundberg

Skyhorse Publishing books may be
purchased in bulk at special discounts for
sales promotion, corporate gifts, fund-
raising, or educational purposes. Special
editions can also be created to
specifications. For details, contact the
Special Sales Department, Skyhorse
Publishing, 307 West 36th Street, 11th
Floor, New York, NY 10018 or info@
skyhorsepublishing.com.

Skyhorse® and Skyhorse Publishing® are
registered trademarks of Skyhorse
Publishing, Inc.®, a Delaware corporation.

www.skyhorsepublishing.com

10 9 8 7 6 5 4 3 2 1

Library of Congress Cataloging-in-
Publication Data is available on file.
Cover design Eric Kang

Print ISBN: 978-1-63220-367-0
Ebook ISBN: 978-1-63450-110-1

Printed in China

TABLE OF CONTENTS

WATER, WATER, EVERYWHERE

It's ubiquitous, yet awe-inspiring. Many agree with me that water is wonderful in most of its incarnations—glinting lakes, or mighty oceans, babbling brooks and rushing rapids, over rocky cliffs or by long stretches of sandy or pebbly beaches. We are drawn to and congregate near water. It exerts a magnetic pull on us, and if we are not fortunate enough to live near it, we are certainly drawn to it in our spare time—to swim, to fish, to boat, or simply to enjoy the view from the shore.

Is it because the sun reflects and sparkles so beautifully on its surface? Or is it the sound of waves lapping delicately or breaking in over land? Surely there's something special in the air, as it's difficult to feel completely depressed on a beautiful day by the sea. Perhaps it connects to our hankering for thrill, adventure, and travel; a boat is a mode of transportation, after all, and probably the only one we use for ornamental purposes in our homes. You won't find a bike or a train on too many people's windowsills—they just don't speak to us the way a sailboat does.

Could it have something to do with life? Water is life, after all—nothing can survive without it. Perhaps we have inherited from time immemorial a gene that instinctively pulls us to water because water equals survival. My homeland of Sweden is a country that features many beautiful areas and magnificent views; living on the waterfront, however, is considered to be the height of luxury. The Swedish Tax Agency agrees on this point and has taken note.

If you love water and associate it with feelings of well-being, happiness, and delight, or even adventure and freedom, it's natural to want to recreate this atmosphere in your home. You don't even have to live near water to get that beachfront feeling. It can be reproduced anywhere to satisfy the yearning in your heart.

My hope is that this book will now inspire you to build, sew, and decorate at home. This is a treasure trove brimming with ideas, tips, and instructions for anyone—landlubber or salty dog—who loves creating beautiful things.

Enjoy!

Editor's note: American units have been added throughout for ease of the user. While every effort has been made to keep the measurements as precise as possible, in some cases the crafter may want to stick with the metric measurements. We leave this up to the judgment of the crafter. When working with wood and sewing quilts, it's best to use exact measurements.

ONE ROOM, THREE NAUTICAL THEMES

Do you have definitive, fixed ideas about what decorating with a nautical motif entails? In your mind's eye, do you see white walls, blue and red highlights, maybe in the image of what can be seen along the coast of New England?

If that is the case, let me show you several ways to decorate a space that's inspired by the sea and the ocean, but still all create their own particular atmosphere and feature different color schemes. While there are more ways to work in the nautical style than what is shown here, as an experiment, I've chosen three main tracks and reworked a single room according to each direction in order to illustrate the wide scope of possibilities available to you.

Nothing is set in stone; the borders are fluid. Some nautical objects, surfaces, and materials can overlap without one style clashing with another. Sometimes they'll meld, and occasionally you might interpret, customize, and adapt ideas to suit your own tastes and preferences, effectively turning your home into a creative expression of you and your family.

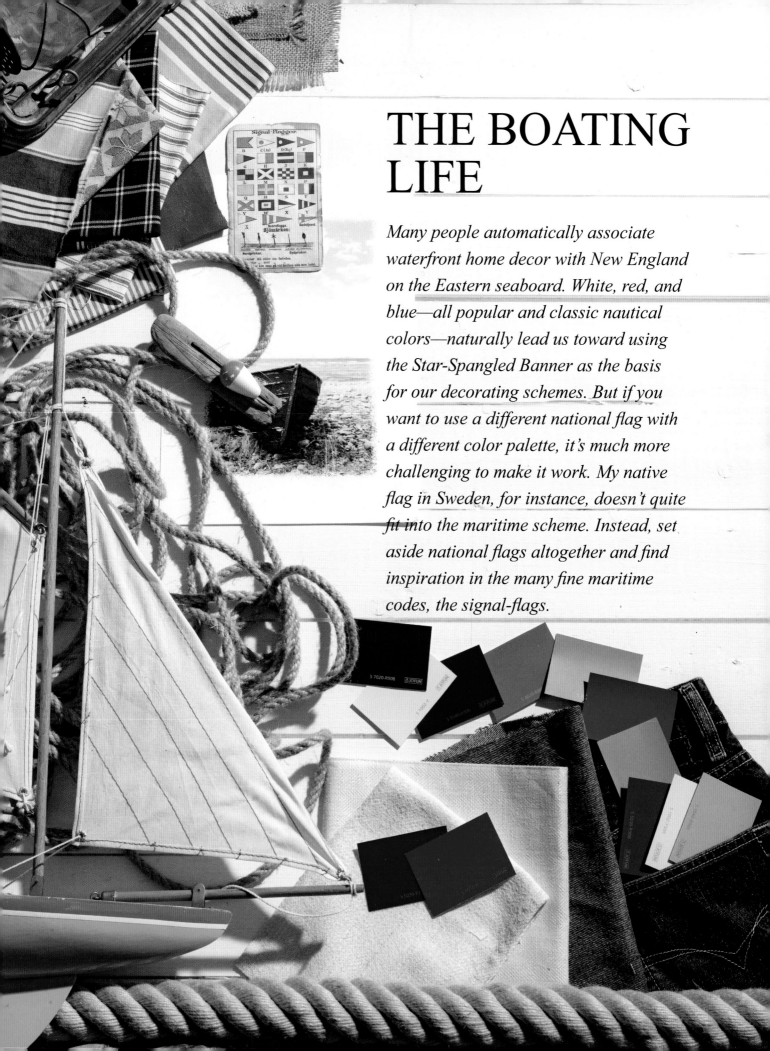

THE BOATING LIFE

Many people automatically associate waterfront home decor with New England on the Eastern seaboard. White, red, and blue—all popular and classic nautical colors—naturally lead us toward using the Star-Spangled Banner as the basis for our decorating schemes. But if you want to use a different national flag with a different color palette, it's much more challenging to make it work. My native flag in Sweden, for instance, doesn't quite fit into the maritime scheme. Instead, set aside national flags altogether and find inspiration in the many fine maritime codes, the signal-flags.

A CLASSIC BACKGROUND
- White painted walls with horizontal panels
- Dark brown wooden floors

There are more variations possible, but this is a safe bet.

YOUR COLOR PALETTE
- White/creamy white
- Red—choose a deep crimson or bright red color
- Blue—dark, navy, or denim blue in different hues

Select muted, slightly darker, or cloudy tones for a more sophisticated look. The trick to making it work is to add:
- Beige linen, rattan/cane, sisal, hemp, etc. Beige adds style and maturity to the whole room by tempering the more vibrant colors.
- Brown & gray can be used with the basic palette to bring out a more genuine feel of nature and reflect more of the outdoors inside.
- Black should be used as an accent to provide an edge.

Yellow is a maritime color that can be difficult to include in a home's color scheme. It is used on signal flags and is sometimes an accent color on the hulls of sailboats. On its own, however—without being featured on a signal flag or sailboat—it is a color that is rarely considered nautical. The same goes for orange, which is prominent on both buoys and safety vests, and green, which is seen on signaling markers.

MATERIALS
Choose natural materials whenever possible. Many boats and accessories are made of fiberglass and plastic, but synthetics do not add a true outdoor feeling.
- Cotton and linen, preferably in a sturdier fabric with more heft and structure
- Basket weave, willow, and rattan/cane
- Sisal and hemp, cords, and hawser-laid rope
- Leather in different brown hues
- Wood—dark-stained, white, black, gray, and driftwood gray
- Stone—an assortment of natural gray hues
- Different types of matte and shiny metals—rusty sheet metal, zinc plate, brass, and chrome

DETAILS THAT WORK ESPECIALLY WELL
- Signal flags
- Boats of all types
- Lighthouses
- Anchors

MAKE CREATIVE USE OF BASKETS

Made of natural materials in handsome hues with roughly textured surfaces, woven baskets in a variety of shapes are great for storage in the nautical home. An everyday leaf-raking basket makes a perfect overhead light, too. It may seem a bit oversized, but it provides just the right contemporary touch. The basket's weave filters and plays with the light, producing beautiful reflections on the ceiling and walls. Search for discounted baskets at shopping outlets and big box stores (the one featured in the picture was just $20). Cut off the handles and drill holes in the bottom for mounting. Add a removable cord protector to the electrical cord to prevent it from scraping against the basket. Cord protectors can be found in the lighting aisle at home improvement stores.

BEACH FRONT

In tropical environments and warmer climates, design inspiration often comes from the beach with its fantastic aquatic fauna and flora— shells, coral reefs, color-saturated fish, and seabirds. If the seashore where you live can't measure up to such exoticism, you can go more low-key with subtler tones. You can still use shells and add a starfish or two for interest, but try to get inspired by the local nature—the beige and gray tones, the softer shades of green, and the deeper blues or grayish blue. Look around you. What is the color palette where you live? This theme is summerlike and is therefore more suited to a cabin or cottage. A way to temper the light, summery ambience to better fit a winter season will be to add more beiges and grays.

COLOR PALETTE
- White/creamy white
- Blue (all colors that make you think of sky and water; the lighter tones are more prominent than the darker ones, which should only be used sparingly)
- Green (emerald green, blue-green, and cool light green tones)
- Turquoise—while bright, striking turquoise is bold and daring, a slightly muted, cloudy version will be easier to match to nature's own colors.

Below is a stylish range of colors sure to suit the coastal aesthetic:
- Beige—linen, rattan, sisal and hemp—beige makes the other colors feel more "mature."
- Grays are useful in that they harmonize with each basic color and add a genuine feel of nature and the outdoors.
- Brown—light and medium tones that are found naturally in the details of wood, basket, and leather.

In warmer latitudes where bright sunshine is a daily feature for most of the year, colors tend to vibrate with more intensity. Be lavish in your use of turquoise, pink, emerald green, orange, and coral red because these colors are found all around in nature. Further north where the climate subdues nature, it's better to use the colors inspired by the colder environment. It may be a little less fun and joyous, but when the interior echoes the outdoors, you get a style in tune with the spirit of your surroundings.

MATERIALS
All natural! This theme is so strongly influenced by our natural environment that no plastics and/or synthetic fabrics should have a place in this setting.
- Cotton and linen, preferably a sturdier weave with marked structure and texture
- Basket weave of willow and rattan/cane, of course, but also straw like that of straw hats
- Sisal and hemp, cords, and hawser rope
- Leather in assorted light and medium tones
- Wood in white, gray, and weathered driftwood gray, as well as assorted light and medium brown tones
- Stone of all hues from white to the darkest gray
- Gray and silver metals of all types, preferably matte or brushed surfaces rather than shiny. A rusty surface will work, but brass can be too yellow.
- By all means use painted and/or peeling surfaces, like objects found while beach combing. Shabby chic charm and furniture with old patina work great here.

DETAILS THAT ADD THAT EXTRA TOUCH:
- Shells and starfish
- Sand and driftwood
- Birds and fish
- Plants—different grasses, succulents, and flowers reminiscent of wildflowers
- Stones—soft, round pebbles that have been polished by the sea and rough-hewn limestone
- Cords, hawser rope, glass buoys and fishing floats, fishing nets—anything that might turn up on the beach

BUILD A COLLECTION OF STRAW HATS

Nothing says summer and sun like a straw hat! Collect several of them and hang them in groups on the wall. They'll not only be eye-catching and beautiful, but will also be close at hand when you need one.

LIKE SAND AND WATER

Light, sun-bleached denim breathes summer and relaxed freedom, so save old, discarded jeans and match them with sturdy linen in beige tones. Watch how quickly a natural friendship emerges.

15

OLD SALTS

This is all about real sailors, the "old salts" who navigate the seven seas. Not for us, the daysailers who bob in the small-boat harbor!

There was a time when large ships were our only means of transport out into the big wide world, the only way to reach other continents. It follows that schooners from the nineteenth century invite us to use a whole different color palette: black as tar, wood in dark brown tones, golden brass, creamy white, and linen beige. Borrow these colors for an elegant and refined nautical interior.

Gain inspiration from the adventurous spirit of the past and its thirst for travel and knowledge—maps and sea charts, vintage books, antique items with the patina of age, and trinkets that speak of foreign shores. It can sometimes be a challenge to mix the old with the new and get it right. However, if you hit the right balance, new modern furniture can be entirely compatible with a nineteenth century dining room set and make an attractive combination. Add a touch of industrial design for an extra, contemporary edge.

PALETTE:

- White/creamy white
- Black (both matte and shiny)
- Brown (medium to dark brown, oiled, hardwood surfaces or clear, lacquered, exotic hardwoods)
- Beige (sand, linen, and yellowed warm beige)
- Grays
- Red, green, turquoise, slate gray to blue—deep, saturated hues, or slightly bleached and a bit grubby, as if aged and worn-out

MATERIALS:

- Cotton, linen, wool, preferably sturdier materials with textured surfaces
- Baskets of willow and rattan/cane
- Sisal, hemp, cord, and hawser rope
- Leather in different medium browns, and tones showing some wear and tear in dark brown and soft blacks.
- Wood in gray, black, and medium/dark brown tones
- Wrought iron metal in dark gray and black, zinc plates, rusty metals, and of course, brass—oxidized and somewhat corroded, or inversely, highly polished.
- Gray sheepskin.

ACCENT DETAILS:

- By all means, use the largest, most exotic shells you can find—perhaps your own treasures or souvenirs from trips to faraway lands.
- Maps, globes, and sea charts
- Vintage books
- Suitcases and trunks
- Old, empty, glass bottles in brown, green, and blue
- Explorers' souvenirs and trinkets suggesting traveling and adventure
- Cords, hawser rope, anchors, compasses, glass buoys, fishing nets—all maritime details that impart authenticity—preferably vintage
- Jolly Rogers, the skull and crossbones—yep, hints of old time piracy
- Scaled down models of older boats, such as gigs and schooners
- Old oil paintings of marine scenes and ships
- Old-fashioned clocks

PATINA

Many useful yet inexpensive decorative items are found in thrift shops and antique stores. They might not be outright nautical in appearance or function, but they can contribute to the general character of the place—vintage books, beer and wine bottles, maps, and oil or kerosene lamps, for example.

Spell it out using old pallet boards to make rough-looking lettering. Cut the boards and leave them uneven. There's no need to sand until their totally smooth; just removing splints and sharp edges with a piece of coarse sandpaper is good enough. Join the letter together with screws fastened on the back of the letter to hide the screw heads. Stain the finished item in gray or white, or slap on some white paint to give it a weathered look.

HAV is Swedish for SEA

PIRATES

Looters and assailants—scary skulls and pirates! There are still enough pirates on the seven seas to get a modern-day Captain Haddock incensed. Skulls come in many shapes and designs, and can add a touch of fun to any room. In fact, borrow a skull from your teen's bedroom if you can. Placed atop a coiled rope inside a round glass bowl or under a glass cloche, it suddenly takes on a more grown-up feel. Slightly menacing and very maritime indeed.

"WATER . . . IT EXERTS A MAGNETIC PULL ON US,
AND IF WE ARE NOT FORTUNATE ENOUGH TO
LIVE NEAR IT, WE ARE CERTAINLY DRAWN TO
IT IN OUR SPARE TIME—TO SWIM, TO FISH,
TO BOAT, OR SIMPLY TO ENJOY
THE VIEW FROM THE SHORE."

A PARTY ON THE COAST

Will this party decor add to your workload and require more of your time? Absolutely!

But for someone who enjoys planning and preparing, this is an integral and pleasurable part of the festivities. The extra thought and effort put into setting the table and decorating won't be lost on your guests. It's not just food that's on the menu but a complete experience that you're sharing with your friends. Furthermore, your decorations are reusable so they can be appreciated again at a later date.

YOU ARE HERE!

Show your guests into the party by welcoming them with a handsome signboard.

Use recycled premade slats of pallet lumber or deck board. It will have the right patina, too, if it has spent some time outside and has become weathered. After a quick once-over with a sander, the wood is clean and ready to be hand-lettered with a brush and some paint.

'Welcome all (ye) friends here, To Captain Graybeard an' his dear'!

CAPTAIN GRAYBEARD INVITES YOU TO THE CAPTAIN'S TABLE

Simple and robust, a long table, benches made of boards placed onto sawhorses, and a woven rag rug for a tablecloth—it's party time at the boathouse! The table setting features red, white, and dark and pale blue, all of which evoke a sense of the lake and the sea. Add that little "extra" something with some well-chosen accessories. Lean a pair of oars in a corner, loop a fishing net along the ceiling, fill a basket or two with cords and ropes, and hoist a lifebuoy up on the wall. The party will turn into a memorable production with you as its stage designer!

BILLOWING SEA OF ROPES

In the middle of the table, set down a tangled skein of ropes in different thicknesses and colors as a table runner. The billowing ropes are beautiful as they are, but can be further embellished with seashells, starfish, glass floats, or other maritime-inspired items that can be easily wedged in between the loops of rope. And there is always room for a boat or two! You can make the most charming small sailboats very simply by using a piece of driftwood, a flowerpot dowel, and pieces of fabric.

A SAILBOAT MADE OF DRIFTWOOD

You'll need a piece of wood, perhaps a piece of driftwood that has been made smooth by the water. Don't be too picky when choosing the shape of the driftwood however, because part of the charm is that just about any piece of wood will become a boat once you've affixed a sail to it.

A small wooden or bamboo flower stake, ¼" (6 mm) in diameter and pointy at one end, makes an excellent mast. In the middle of the boat, drill a hole for the mast of the same diameter as the flower stake and approximately ½" (1 cm) deep. Cut the mast to desired height. Drill a small hole through the mast just less than 1" (2 cm) from the lower end of the mast and another small hole at about 1 ⅜" to 2" (3–4 cm) from the top. Use any size drill between #47–53 (1½ to 2 mm) in diameter. Drill a small hole at each end of the boat. Glue on the mast.

Cut out simple triangle sails from crisply starched cotton fabric. Rig the sail onto the mast with the aid of a thin metal thread (see picture for detail). If it's too difficult to pierce the fabric with the metal thread, use a pin first to poke a hole. Straighten and tighten the metal thread and wind the ends to fasten. Cut out a small pennant from the crisply starched fabric and glue it to the top of the mast. (See how to crisp starch fabric on p. 26.)

hole

PARTY BUNTING

Bunting makes for pure party magic! Hang a long strand of little colorful pennants, and suddenly the atmosphere turns more festive and happy. The garlands in the boathouse are made out of fabric from the stash box, but when you want a whole lot of bunting to put together, it takes far too long to stitch all of them. Instead, starch the material from the stash (see detailed description below) to make it possible to cut the flags directly to desired shape and size. Fold some fabric bias tape or cotton ribbon in half lengthwise and press with an iron. Place the folded ribbon/tape around the flag's upper edge and machine stitch it in place with a large zigzag stitch. Place the pennants close together along the ribbon/tape and continue until you've attached them all.

GRASS LOOKS GREAT

Old pots perk up with new life when you give them a few strokes with a paintbrush. Decorate them with painted text on a strip of coarse linen fabric—coordinates for longitude and latitude are perfect for a seafaring theme.

Use stencils for the lettering (see page 142 for instructions). Cut the fabric strip slightly wider than the letters you're using, and slightly more than 1" (3 cm) longer than the pot's circumference. Paint the fabric white, too, and a bit haphazardly as well to bring out the fabric's texture. Let dry. Pull a few strands of thread loose along the fabric's long sides to make it unravel a little, fringe-like. When the lettering is dry, brush the back of the fabric with some hobby glue and stick the fabric onto the pot.

Fluttering bunches of tall grasses are by far the most charming potted flower for a beach party. You can get ornamentals at a garden center, but a clump of dug-up wild-growing grass will do just as well.

HOW TO CRISP-STARCH FABRIC

Spread out a piece of oilcloth or plastic on your worktable for protection. Brush both sides of all fabric pieces with wallpaper paste or any type of PVA craft glue until thoroughly damp. Pin them up to dry on a makeshift drying line made of string. Once the glue has dried, the fabric will be completely stiff, but you will still be able to cut through it. You can still iron the glue-treated fabric, but put the fabric between some used cotton sheets to protect the ironing board and the iron from the glue.

PINCHED BY A LIFE PRESERVER

With some added paint, wooden curtain rings make nice little life preservers, which are, of course, perfect to use as nautical napkin rings.

Pinch off all metal fixtures on the rings. Sand the surface smooth with fine sandpaper and wipe clean with a rag dipped in a cleaning fluid such as denatured ethanol. Then paint the rings white and let them dry. Once dry, paint four wide bands in red or blue across the ring.

STEADY SEA LEGS

Common saucers make fine holders for pillar candles. Use a small saucer for one candle or larger platter-sized ones for groupings. Raise the saucer and make it stylish by gluing on hardwood balls (available in hobby stores). The larger they are, the edgier your candle holder will look! Use a two-part adhesive and then paint the saucer with matte, water-based paint. Decorate around the candle with seashells, sand, or small, pretty pebbles.

GLEAMING GLASS

Seek out old-fashioned bottles in glimmering blue and green at thrift stores. They make the finest candleholders for next to nothing. Pour some water into the bottle and simply add a common tall, tapered candle.

"IT'S NOT SIMPLY FOOD ON THE PARTY MENU—IT'S A WHOLE EXPERIENCE THAT YOU'RE SHARING."

27

PILE UP THE STONES

Don't overcomplicate things. Use what you find close by for decoration.
A popular pastime on the stone-strewn beaches of the coast is to build stone
pillars, the higher the better. Decorate your table with small stone pillars.

WINDY WEATHER

Add some heft to glasses by attaching a small stone to the stems with some
wound twine. The glasses remain steady, and the stones make a fun decoration
from the beach.

FRISKY BREEZE

Naturally, we prefer to sit outside whenever possible; only really nasty weather
will keep us from enjoying summer at its fullest. If it's unusually windy, however, several tried and true ways keep table settings from flying off.

Knot the tablecloth in place so the wind can't lift it. Wrap twine around a
hefty stone and place the stone on the ground next to the table. Knot the other
end of the twine around the corner of the tablecloth. Use one stone for each table
corner.

FESTIVE FLAGS

Stylish finger foods or decorated cupcakes? Pretty flags work every time. They're
extremely simple to make in colors and patterns that match the theme of the
party.

Start with thin wooden grilling skewers. Cut a fabric rectangle measuring
approximately 1 ½" x 4" (3 ½ cm x 10 cm) and brush the back of it with white
PVA glue. Fold the fabric in half around the end of the skewer and glue the fabric
together. Once the glue has dried, the fabric will be stiff but still pliable enough
to be scissored into shapes, such as a flag with two points (also called a
"swallow-tail") or a three-sided pennant.

TO CATCH A PIRATE

A whole gang of pirates awaits playful party guests. This beach game is so much fun to put together from wood and hemp rope, simply because the cheerfully striped pirates are so handsome and strong.

YOU'LL NEED THE FOLLOWING ITEMS FOR EACH PIRATE:

- Lumber, measuring 2" x 2" (45 mm x 45 mm) and 2 ⅓' (70 cm) long
- 1 wooden ball, 3" (7 cm) in diameter
- 1 fluted dowel pin, ⅜" (10 mm) in diameter
- Acrylic paint in black, white, and marine colors

HOW TO:

1. With an axe or a handsaw, sharpen one end of the lumber to a point to make it easy to secure the pirate into the ground. Drill a hole at the other end of the lumber, ⅜" (10 mm) in diameter and ¾" (2 cm) in depth. Repeat the drilling in the wooden ball. Sand it smooth and round off any sharp corners and edges.

2. Use acrylic paint (craft paint or whatever paint you have at home) to paint the top for the pirate's white sweater first. Paint the bottom in black (the pirate's pants). Once the paint has dried, apply 1" (25 mm) wide masking tape to the sweater part to make it striped. Paint a second coat of white for the sweater and let dry. This white coat seals the masking tape and makes your stripes perfect. Then paint the more colorful stripes. Remove the masking tape.

3. Paint the pirate's head by hand. First make an outline in pencil of a black bandanna around the head, an eye patch, the other eye, and mouth. Use a brush, or for ease, a Sharpie, and knot a fabric bandanna around the pirate's head instead of painting one.

4. Insert the fluted dowel pin into the painted "pirate" body. Use wood or hobby glue to attach the pirate head (see page 31). Give each pirate a number. Our game has three pirates for five points, two pirates for ten points, and one single for a full twenty-five points. Paint the numbers freehand or use a stencil.

5. *Rings:* Tossing rings are made from sturdy rope, preferably hemp, just under ¾" (18–20 mm) thick.

Each ring requires approximately 3' (90 cm) of rope. Bend the rope into a circle and glue the surface of each end together with a hot glue gun (sets quickly). To strengthen the bond, take a strip of material measuring approximately 2" x 12" (5 cm x 15 cm), and wind it around the rope junction. Fasten with some contact adhesive. A quick shortcut: Tape the junction with duct tape.

THE MOST BEAUTIFUL BUCKET

A common, utilitarian tool becomes the finest ornamental container. A galvanized bucket can be used as a cooler for drinks, a vase for flowers, or simply as a bucket of water with a towel and a bar of soap for guests to rinse off their hands. Dress up a plain bucket for the party on the coast with a piece of burlap.

Paint the burlap almost completely white. Pull out threads along the edges so they unravel into a straggly fringe. Paint letters and numbers on the burlap with stencils (see page 142). Our bucket says N52°, but any compass point will work. For outside use, glue the fabric onto the bucket with waterproof wood glue.

BOAT PIN SECURES NAPKINS

When the wind is high and our sails are full, a clothespin helps secure the napkin to the rim of the plate.

Use a small piece of driftwood for the boat hull. Place a piece of sandpaper onto the worktable and sand the hull flat by working it back and forth across the sandpaper. Glaze it with craft paint diluted with water. Use a 4" (10 cm) stiff metal wire as boat mast, such as iron craft wire found at craft and florist supply stores, of 14 or 16 gauges (1 ½ mm in diameter). Drill a hole in the hull for the mast. Glue the boat onto a clothes peg.

Cut the sail out of a piece of crisply starched cotton fabric. Poke the metal wire through the fabric and glue the mast to the hull with a drop of superglue. For a pennant, cut a long fabric rectangle, about ½" x 2 ⅜" (1 ½ cm x 6 cm). Brush PVA glue on the back of the fabric, fold it in half around the mast, and glue the backs together. Once the glue has dried, use a pair of scissors to cut the end of the pennant to a point.

approx. 2" (5 cm)

approx. 2 3/4" (7 cm)

6" (15 cm)

PALLET
PATINA

Discarded pallets and reused lumber slats can be transformed into charming decorative items. Their weather-beaten patina is a bonus.

You can certainly create a wooden picture from scratch with new materials if you wish, but the beauty of using pallet lumber or deck boards is that half of the work is already done. Precut and nailed squares of pallet lumber measuring 32" x 32" (80 cm x 80 cm) become "canvases" ready for your artwork. All you have to do is split them to your preferred size, and sand and smooth the surfaces before picking up your paint and brushes.

ORNAMENTAL BOARDS

Slightly warped and weather-beaten boards are often so beautiful in their own right that they don't need much in the way of embellishment to make an interesting picture. Try coating the boards with diluted white paint to get a glaze-like effect, and then attach different kinds of objects with adhesives or nails. Coarse hemp ropes with hefty knots and a small wooden boat from a souvenir shop are examples. Or why not a fishing net, a float, a starfish, an exquisite shell, or a piece of driftwood?

ARTFUL

You don't have to be the next Picasso to create a picture! Beige for sand, dark-blue for the sea and a lighter blue for the sky—even if your representation only consists of three shambolic lines, everybody will make the connection. If you want to take it a step further, you can add a few dots of white with a sponge for the clouds in the sky or a few strokes of lighter paint to put some whitecaps on the waves. If you want to include some real sand into the picture, simply paint a small amount of PVA glue onto the beige area and dust over it with some sand. But keep it simple. It's the surrounding items that will pull that feeling of the sea and the beach together.

How about some nautical stripes? First, paint all your boards white, and then paint every second board in one of your chosen colors. Once the paint is dry, sand the painted boards until they have that worn and weathered look. Stripes are plenty nautical in and of themselves, but if you wish to gussy them up a bit, add some decor or lettering to them. (For more on painting with stencils, see page 142.)

SIGNPOSTS—HERE AND THERE

Are they necessary? Not really, but lettered way signs can be both fun and interesting to incorporate as design elements. Pallet wood makes fine nautical signs to be hung one over the other, affixed with hemp rope and intricate knot work.

We chose to use a brown stain and lettered maritime directional signs for all rooms in the house. The living room becomes the "Salon," the dining room the "Mess Hall," the kitchen the "Cook's Galley," and the bedroom a "Cabin."

The same idea can be accomplished with white and wonderful blue and green tones that feature your choice of words reminiscent of the ocean and the beach.

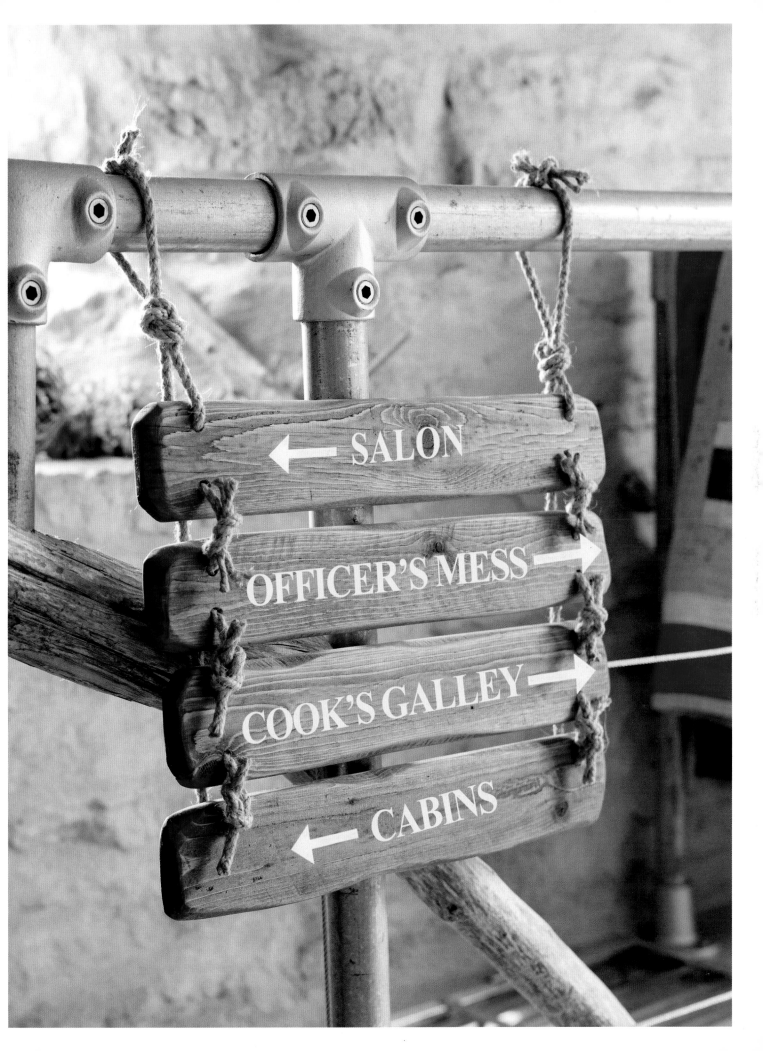

SIGNALING SIGNS

A large signal flag can give an edgy effect all by itself. Use a pre-fabricated slat of pallet lumber or deck board and remove two to three boards so it's not absolutely square. Sand it and stain it in your chosen color. You can use any glaze as long as it´s not waxy or oily. Dark, saturated brown is a good choice for a background tone. It is reminiscent of old boats and makes a fine contrast to signal flags that typically do not contain any brown at all.

It's effective to let the background color come through in the joints between the different fields of color in the signal flag. It's also quicker to achieve, since all colors can be painted in one go instead of in layers. Select a narrow masking tape and tape up the flag you intend to paint (see diagrams for different signal flags on page 50). Press down hard on the tape to make it stick. Paint your flag with acrylic paints in two or three coats. While the last coat of paint is still wet, remove the tape.

BOARDS ALIGNED

Whether wide, narrow, short, long, thick, or thin, boards can be joined together in a long row just like a folding screen. This acts like a shutter on the windowsill or a decorative background for other nautical objects.

The boards are left uneven at the top, but trimmed flat at the bottom so that they're flush with the ground and steady when standing.

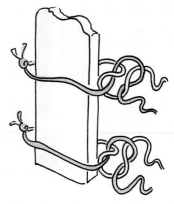

Use coarse hemp string and carry it all along the front and back of the boards. After each board, pull the string tight and make a knot. The distance of the knot itself gives you enough slack to fold up the boards.

Leave the boards as they are, or whitewash or stain them. If you want to copy the picture, paint the boards with water-based white primer first and then apply a blue coat of acrylic paint. Once the paint is completely dry, sand the surface until almost all the blue paint has come off and the white paint shows in patches allowing the natural wood to peek through here and there.

"ONE MAN'S TRASH IS ANOTHER MAN'S TREASURE!"

SALVAGING BOARDS

Old lumber from pallets, decking, and fences, any odds and ends of boards thrown in a pile—all materials are battered by weather and wind if left outside. They will soak up water and then dry out again in the sun, which creates small cracks and fissures on their surface that leaves a nice patina not so easily faked.

You can hurt yourself on splintery boards. Rugged, coarse surfaces are dust magnets and they're next to impossible to dust. So how can we remedy all this without losing the charm we're after? Gravel and the occasional forgotten rusty nail make these planks an absolute no-no in the carpenter's workshop with its planes and band saws—only manual power tools work here! It´s cheaper to replace the blades in a regular jigsaw.

HOW TO:

1. If you have a whole pallet, use a jigsaw to cut the longest pieces possible out of the boards without any attached nails.

2. If you want the boards to have that real "driftwood" appearance, roughen up the boards a bit by making the cuts choppy. Making a few deep grooves or cutting the edges with a knife will also impart some of the desired character.

3. Sand the boards with a sander using a medium grit sandpaper. Don't worry, sanding won't make the boards look new. They'll still have a visibly rough surface. Sand them just enough to remove splinters and make them less spiky to the touch, which is enough for ornamental items. Or sand them down really smooth for more user-friendly objects.

4. The wood will take on a grayer or deeper tone if it's stained with a glaze. Choose a natural looking grayish tone.

5. One or two coats of white colorwash give the wood a bright appearance without hiding the grain and desirable wood feel. Use acrylic paint diluted with plenty of water for this.

6. Try the lighter touch. Simply brush the wood lightly with undiluted white acrylic paint using an almost dry brush. It lightens the color of the wood and draws attention to the unevenness of the rugged surface.

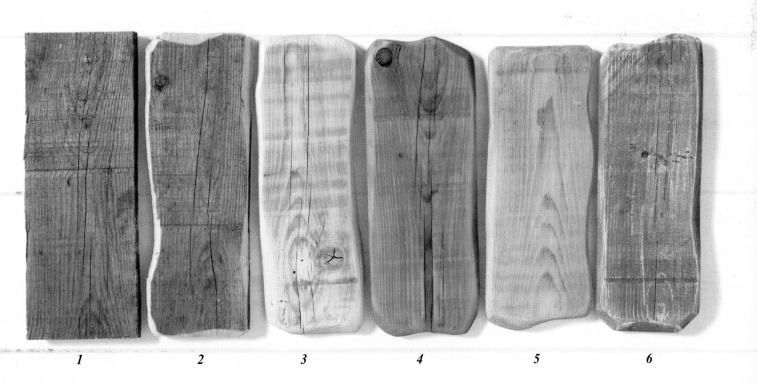

1   *2*   *3*   *4*   *5*   *6*

SIGNALS GALORE

When boats need to communicate with anyone within range, they hoist signal flags. There are individual signal flags for each letter and number, but single flags can also carry complete messages. However, you don't need to know how to decipher those messages to appreciate the flags' festive look and their decorative aspect.

SANDED SIGNALS

Discarded old boards and wooden odds and ends make excellent raw material for a vertical signal flag display.

Smooth the surfaces with a sander until soft and stain in a background tone. I used brown as it makes me think of old boats. Paint signal flags with acrylic paint from the craft store (see instructions for chest of drawers on page 44). When the paint is dry, sand the pieces of wood with sandpaper to achieve a weather-beaten look. To attach signal flags vertically in a row, screw in two eyelets on one side of the boards and two hooks on the other side, so the boards hook onto one another. At the top attach a piece of nice driftwood and hang the boards from it.

COUCH CUSHION SIGNALS

Signal flags make perfect motifs for cushions! Sew nautical style cushions for next to nothing compared to what you would pay for them in a trendy home-furnishing store.

HOW TO:

1. The instructions for the cushion covers are more or less identical to those for the table mats on page 45, except the signal flag's dimensions changes to 16" x 20" (40 cm x 50 cm). For this size, use a 20" x 20" down cushion to make it a firm and puffy cushion.

2. For an authentic, durable exterior, choose sturdy cotton and linen fabrics. Use heavy-duty sewing thread to sew decorative topstitching along the seams on the different fabric patches for a professional-looking finish.

3. Make zippered openings on the back of the cushion covers for easy removal (see denim cushion covers on page 75).

SMALL SIGNALS

Use any sized signal flag, large to small, to create your own, nautical-themed wall art.

Here's a cut and paste project that even the younger members of your family can try their hand at.

Write up a small, art gallery-style label for each flag showing the letter it stands for, along with a word starting with that letter; S as in seasick, M as in Marine, O for Ocean, B for beaches…

HOW TO:

1. Use a shadow box or, as seen in the picture, a small drawer found in a thrift store. Paint the box and cover the bottom with nautical-themed paper or a sea chart for the background.

2. Using scissors or an X-acto knife, cut out approximately 2" x 2 ½" (5 cm x 6 ½ cm) pieces of cardboard to use as backing material for the signal flags. Check your fabric stash for lightweight cotton swatches in appropriate colors or use colored paper. A single color works well, but you'll create a more dynamic look if the fabric has a small print overall. Use diagrams for the signal flags (see page 50) and scale them to fit the size of the cardboard cutouts. A regular glue stick works fine for both fabric and paper. To achieve a free-floating, three-dimensional effect, use foam mounting pads to attach the flags in the shadow box.

FLAGS AHEAD

Go full steam ahead and make a whole collage of signal flags. A plain piece of furniture can transform an entire room. A chest of drawers that oozes strong maritime influences is a strong focal point, allowing the rest of the decorations to be more subtle and still get the message through.

"A CHEST OF DRAWERS THAT EXUDES STRONG MARITIME INFLUENCES IS A STRONG FOCAL POINT. . ."

HOW TO:

1. The wooden chest of five drawers featured in this picture is IKEA's "Tarva" model and is made in plain pine with no finish on the surface. Stain the formerly bare wood in a shade of your choice (I used a gray shade). If your chest of drawers has an old finish that needs to be covered up instead, sand the surfaces and wash down with a product such as trisodium phosphate (TSP). Then go ahead and paint it with only a primer. Zinsser is a great choice. It blocks any bleeding from previous staining and gives good coverage. The primer can be tinted in a nice shade if you want something other than white. You don't need to paint nicely and evenly, as the surface will be lightly sanded afterwards, which will give a nice, smooth surface. Even the area to be decorated with flags needs a base coat of primer or stain.

2. Use the signal flag diagrams on page 50 to calculate the size of the individual flags and colored fields needed. You might have to recalculate their sizes to accommodate your particular piece of furniture, which might make the flags look either a bit thicker or more elongated. Not to worry—they will still look like signal flags even if the proportions are a little off.

3. Sketch the flags' placement lightly with a pencil, and tape along the edges with masking tape. Press the tape down hard along the edges to seal off the paint.

4. Use acrylic paint from the craft store or any acrylic paint leftovers you might have. First paint each flag with an all-over coat of the lightest color. Repeat the coating if needed and let them dry thoroughly. Sketch the flag's darker areas lightly and again seal off with masking tape. Paint the darker colors.

5. If you paint the front of drawers, you can fool the eye into thinking that each flag is a drawer. Make a deep indent with a screwdriver on the border between two flags. The indent has to be deep enough to scratch the wood. Add shadowing by rubbing a graphite pencil in the scratch.

6. Freshly painted surfaces can end up a little too polished and plastic looking, so sand the decorated surfaces with fine sandpaper, not to age the furniture but to flatten the sheen, making it appear a bit used and softening the look. Finish off with a clear, water-based, non-yellowing sealer or just rub the surfaces with clear beeswax, which has a nice scent as well!

7. To fool someone into thinking that each flag is the front of a separate drawer, put a knob or handle on each flag. This could quickly become pricey, but luckily there are inexpensive alternatives that also add some extra marine effect. A sturdy leather belt can be cut up in bits and turned into several handles. If the belt is wide, halve it lengthwise to make even more.

8. For each handle, cut a piece of leather belt measuring at least 4¾" x ⅝"–1" (12–14 cm x 15–25 mm). Using scissors, make the edges slightly rounded. Sand the edges and the upper surface with finely grained sandpaper, which will soften the leather and give the handle a slightly used look. Drill a hole at both ends about ½" (1 ½ cm) measured from the short end.

9. Attach the leather handles, complete with washers. You'll get the nicest look with round head brass screws even though the washers are usually silver. Measure the distance between the drilled holes in the leather handle. Mark and drill holes into the wood of the drawer about ½" (1 ½ cm) shorter than between the holes in the leather. This will ensure that the piece of leather billows outwards, leaving room for your fingers to grab the handle.

SIGNAL FLAGS MAKE A SMART TABLE SETTING

Whip up some nautical tablemats. Mix and match! With such a vast variety of flags out there, there is no need to repeat yourself— different flags can be used all around the table.

HOW TO:

1. The placemats need to be sturdy to keep their shape, so you'll need to use heavyweight fabric in single colors with a surface structure that gives it character. Discarded jeans and sturdy linen towels from the thrift store are tailor-made for this!

2. Use the diagram for the signal flags on page 50. Tweak the measurements to fit a placemat size of approximately 14" x 19" (35 x 47 cm). Sketch the pattern and sew by following Step 1 of the simple quilted throw on page 47.

3. Cut a backing in the same size as the flag. Use sturdy fabric here, too.

4. Place the front and back pieces of the fabric together, right sides facing each other, and stitch them together along the four sides, leaving an opening of about approximately 9" (20 cm) along one side. Trim off excess fabric across the corners, turn the mat inside out, and iron.

5. For a professional, clean-looking finish, use heavy-duty sewing thread for decorative topstitching along the outer edges and to outline the different color blocks.

SAY IT WITH SIGNAL FLAGS

A quilted throw made entirely of signal flags is a labor of love that will be appreciated by the whole family. It makes a nice cozy blanket to use after frequent dips in the lake or ocean, a lovely travel quilt to bring on boat trips or picnics, or a great throw for the couch when you decorate with a nautical theme in mind.

This quilt calls for fabric in more muted shades of colors, featuring a pale blue denim background for the flags, and a slightly coarser linen fabric for the edging. You can use solid colors throughout if you wish, but you'll add a touch of fun and energy if the cotton fabric has a small overall print. I confess that somehow I managed to turn one flag upside down. Oops! But I believe in my heart that only true old salts would notice which one it is…

46

QUILTED SIGNAL FLAG THROW

Overall size: approximately 67" x 73" (171 cm x 186 cm)

Seam allowance: ¾" (1 cm) is included in all measurements.

MATERIALS:

Flags: lightweight cotton fabric

Flags, inside backing: 25 pieces, each approximately 6 ¾" x 8" (17 cm x 20 cm) of lightweight cotton fabric (This fabric will not show, so an old cotton sheet will work just fine.)

Flags, extra batting: 25 pieces, each approximately 6" x 7" (15 cm x 18 cm) of thin quilt batting. This is just a filling to give the flag a nice structure. Lofty polyester batting can easily be torn apart, making one thick layer into two thinner pieces.

Batting, the whole quilt: approximately 55" x 100" (140 cm x 250 cm) of thin quilt batting (found at craft and fabric stores or on the website Quilt Batting Plus at www.quiltbattingplus.com).

Background fabric (area around the flags): 53" x 59" (135 cm x 150 cm)

Quilt backing: 55" x 61" (140 cm x 155 cm) coarse linen, sturdy cotton, or lightweight denim fabric

Border: Beige linen or cotton fabric, 11" x 59" (28 cm x 150 cm) and red linen or cotton fabric, 63" x 59" (160 cm x 150 cm)

Corner squares: 4 pieces, 7 ½" x 7 ½" (19 cm x 19 cm) of denim fabric

Binding: 5 strips of lightweight cotton fabric (I used blue), 4" x 59" (10 cm x 150 cm)

TO CUT:

Batting: Cut one large piece measuring approximately 54" x 60" (137 cm x 152 cm). Also, cut 6 strips measuring 7" x 55" (18 cm x 140 cm).

Background fabric: 30 strips, 4 ¾" x 7 ⅞" (12 cm x 20 cm) + 6 strips, 4 ¾" x 54" (12 cm x 137 cm)

Border: Beige: four strips, 2 ¾" x 59" (7 cm x 150 cm) Red: four strips (A), 5 ½" x 59" (14 x 150 cm) + five strips (B), 7 ½" x 59" (19 x 150 cm)

HOW TO:

Stitch all seams with right sides together unless instructed otherwise.

1. Draw the flags using the diagram of the completed flags as your guide. Add a seam allowance of ¾" (1 cm) to each piece needed for a flag. Not all flags need to be pieced together from several different pieces of fabric. For some flags, start by cutting out a whole flag in the flag's background color measuring 6 ¾" x 7 ⅞" (17 cm x 20 cm) including seam allowance, and then finish the flag by appliquéing the other pieces on top. It is easier to do this if there is an X or a cross on the flag (as shown in illustrations M, R, V, X) or just a small square (P and S). It is easier to make a paper pattern for squares that contain triangles or have points, and use it when cutting out the shapes.

2. Stitch the pieces together for the different flags. Piece them together by placing the wrong sides together. Add a piece of inside backing and a piece of batting in between the two layers of fabric. Center the batting between the layers. Pin the pieces together. Quilt the piece together by topstitching along the seams. Use a zigzag stitch around the flag's outer edge to hold the layers of fabric together. Press the flag.

3. Place the pressed flags on a large table and move the flags around until you're satisfied with the design. Attach the flags to the background material. Use the shorter strips, which are the same length as the long side of the flag. Stitch strips of background fabric and flags

together, alternating between the two until you have a band consisting of five flags and six strips. Each band starts and ends with a strip of background fabric. Press the seam allowances onto the back side of the background fabric.

4. Now stitch together the flag bands using the long strips of background fabric until you have a piece with five rows of flags and six strips of background fabric. Press the seam allowances onto the back side of the background fabric.

5. Now it's time to set in the batting and line the quilt with the backing fabric. Place the flag piece that you've sewn together against the quilt's backing fabric with wrong sides together and place the batting in between the layers of fabric. This is a big quilt and a bit awkward to handle and machine stitch, so it's important to baste (hand stitch) carefully along the sides and also crisscross large baste stitches all over and through the large surface of flags.

6. Stitch a zigzag seam all around the outside edges of the piece. Then quilt by topstitching (straight stitch 4) along the edges of all background fabric strips (see the broken lines on the quilt diagram).

7. The quilt should now measure 54" x 60" (137 cm x 152 cm) but will become larger when you add a padded border all around the centerpiece.

8. **Border:** Join the beige strips by stitching along the short ends into one really long strip. Repeat the process with the red A strips. Press all seam allowances open. Stitch the two super long strips together on the long side. Press the seam allowance onto the back of the beige fabric.

9. Now cut the bicolored strip into four lengths of 54" (137 cm) + 60" (152 cm). Attach two denim fabric corner squares by stitching them to the short ends of the longest strips measuring 60" (152 cm).

10. Stitch to join the red B strips into one long strip and cut this into two lengths of 54" (137 cm) + two lengths of 73" (186 cm).

11. Pin the shorter bicolor strips along the quilt's short sides, right side against right side. Turn the quilt and

pin the single-colored, same length B strip against the back of the quilt, right sides together. Stitch the strips to the quilt.

12. Using long stitches, baste the strips of batting to the border strips' seam allowances. Then turn the border strips down and place them together, wrong sides together, with the batting in between. Press. Use zigzag stitching to sew/hold the strips together along the outer edge. Quilt the border by topstitching along both long sides of the beige strip.

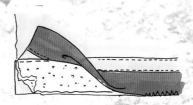

13. Repeat this process to attach the border with denim squares along the remaining sides of the quilt's centerpiece.

14. **Binding:** Stitch the 4" wide strips together along the short ends to make one long strip. Press the seam allowances open at the joining seams. Fold the strip in half lengthwise, wrong sides together. Press. Stitch the binding along the edges of the quilt border, placing the binding on the backside of the quilt. Use ⅝" (1½ cm) seam allowance. Press the seam allowance towards the binding strip. Then fold the binding around the quilt edge and press it down onto the quilt's front side. Stitch the binding on with a topstitch along the binding's folded edge.

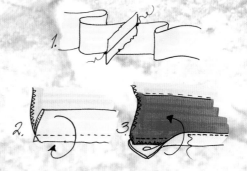

POTHOLDERS

These handsome pot holders will come in handy if we're lucky on the next fishing trip . . .

HOW TO:

1. A signal flag makes a great potholder. Its inside padding needs to be made of a heat-resistant material. A discarded wool blanket or the wool sweater that shrunk in the wash works well. Cut to 7 ½" x 8 ¾" (19 cm x 22 cm).

2. Calculate a finished size of approximately 7 ½" x 8 ¾" (19 cm x 22 cm). Add at least 1" (2 cm) extra seam allowance all around. It's easy to get things muddled, so draw a proper paper pattern to help calculate the measurement for each piece that needs to be cut. Add seam allowances around each piece (bearing in mind that the allowance needs to be 1" on the outline of the flag). Cut and stitch the pieces together for the flag.

3. Cut a backing, approximately 9" x 10 ¼" (23 cm x 26 cm) for the potholder. Place the padding on top and fold in the edges all around. Press. Fold the edges on the flag the same way and pin the flag and the backing together. Stitch them together with double topstitch all around the edges. Quilt the potholder by making a decorative topstitch along the seams, contrasting the flags' different color fields.

4. Join two belt loops from a pair of discarded jeans together lengthwise to make a loop that you can hang it with. If you find it too awkward to stitch such thick material, a cotton ribbon will work just fine.

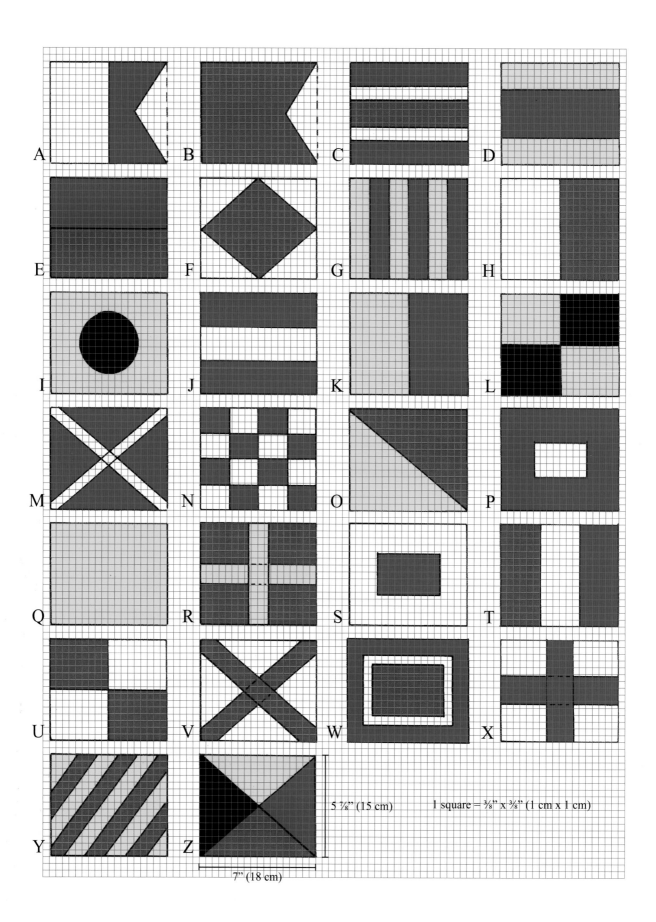

A   B   C   D

E   F   G   H

I   J   K   L

M   N   O   P

Q   R   S   T

U   V   W   X

Y   Z

5 ⅞" (15 cm)   1 square = ⅜" x ⅜" (1 cm x 1 cm)

7" (18 cm)

A BEACHY BEDROOM

Tongue-and-groove wood and cross beams add an atmosphere of beachfront living. Perhaps you dream of covering the entire wall in tongue and groove or wood paneling. It's far simpler and quicker, however, to fudge things a little. A generously sized homemade headboard is all that's required to achieve that beachfront effect in the bedroom.

You can save precious money by doing some woodwork and building a headboard with a nautical twist instead of purchasing a ready-made one. I exaggerated its size somewhat and made it really tall to ensure that it's the first thing one notices in the room and that it imparts a nautical feel to the whole space.

The advantage of building the headboard yourself is that if you get tired of it or have to move, you can simply unscrew it and remove it from the wall.

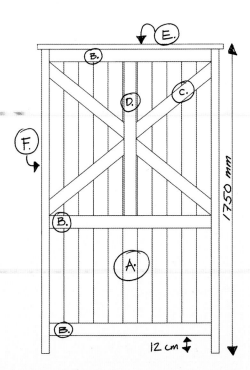

HEADBOARD

Size: For bed sizes Single/Queen/King
Width of headboard: 40"/69"/79" (1040 mm/1750 mm/2000 mm)
Height of headboard: 68 ½" (1740 mm)

MATERIALS:

Please note that measurements given for furring strips and framing studs are the common sizes used by the lumber yard. The project is designed around the actual size, which is slightly smaller.

- A - 1/2/2 sheets of plywood, untreated wood siding:
  $^9/_{16}$ x 48" x 96" (14 x 122 x 244 mm)
- B - 3 cross rails:
  Inches: 1" x 3" (all sizes) x 35 $^7/_8$"/63 $^7/_8$"/73 $^7/_8$"
  Millimeter: 19 x 65 x 935 mm/1615 mm/1873 mm
- C - 4 cross braces, furring strip:
  Inches: 1" x 3" x 22 $^{15}/_{16}$"/32 $^3/_8$"/37 $^1/_8$"
  Millimeters: 19 mm x 65 mm x 583 mm/822 mm/943 mm
- D - 1 center stile:
  Inches: 1" x 3" x 33 $^7/_8$"
  Millimeters: 19 mm x 65 mm x 860 mm
- E - 1 top rail:
  Inches: 1" x 4" x 42 ½"/70 ½"/80 $^1/_3$"
  Millimeters: 19 mm x 89 mm x 1080 mm/1790 mm/2040 mm
- F - 2 stiles, framing studs:
  Inches: 2" x 3" x 67 ¾"
  Millimeters: 40 mm 65 mm x 1720 mm
- Wood glue
- Wood screws with flat head, length: 1 or 1 $^1/_8$" + 2" + 3"

TOOLS:

- Power drill
- Circular saw
- This woodworking project will be much more enjoyable and simpler if you have a good table saw with an adjustable miter cutting feature.

53

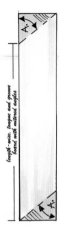

HOW TO'S:

1. Construction lumber is often stored at below ambient temperature at building supply stores, so once you've brought it home, lay it flat in an area with good air circulation to dry out the wood for a few weeks before starting the project. Optimal conditioning takes longer, but a short curing spell is better than none at all.

2. For a single-size bedboard, cut wood siding W 35 ⅞" x H 63" (91 cm x 160 cm). For the larger sizes, join the two sheets of wood siding and cut to a measurement W 63 ⅞" x H 63" (161 cm x 160 cm) for the Queen and W 73 ⅞" x H 63" (187 cm x 160 cm) for the King. Cut the wood siding accordingly. You need to make very clean and even cuts, so clamp a board along your markings and use it for support when sawing.

3. Cut all the rails from furring strips according to measurements above. The cross braces are cut to size at the same time they're being mitered, as follows: Angle A, 64°/72°/74° (see diagram at top left).

4. The sturdy stiles are the headboard's legs. To make room for the skirting board around the floor, saw a notch in the back of one end of the stiles. The notch is made at the same height and depth as the skirting board.

5. Sand the wood down on all pieces so it's nice and smooth. Sharp edges are beveled and rounded. Shellac all the knots to prevent them from bleeding or coming through. Paint all the cut pieces once. For a white headboard, prime first with white primer. All other shades can be painted without a primer and instead use the topcoat as first coat after diluting it a little so it acts more like a stain and will be absorbed by the wood. DO NOT shellac the knots if you want to stain the wood! Do one coat of stain. When the lumber in the finished headboard has dried a bit more, you'll avoid cracks where the wood color emerges, as the entire surface has been painted.

6. Place the wood siding flat on the floor. Brush some glue onto the back of two rails (B) and place them across the upper and lower edge of the siding. Leave heavy weights on top of the rails while they dry—piles of heavy books work well. Repeat the procedure with the centerstile, the four cross braces, and finally, the last cross rail just underneath the cross braces.

7. Once the glue has dried, turn the headboard carefully so the back faces you. Reinforce the glue by screwing the siding onto the rails, the center stile, and the cross braces with short wood screws.

8. Turn the headboard again so this time the front side is upwards. Place the side stiles (F) on end alongside the headboard's long edges. The stiles' upper ends need to be flushed with the headboard's upper edge, while the stiles' lower ends exceed the bottom of the headboard by 4 ¾" (12 cm). Screw the stiles into the short ends of the cross rails using your longest screws. Mark the placing of the short ends of the cross rails. Predrill holes through the side stiles. The center of the holes should be 1" measured from the back side. Brush some glue along the side edge of the wood siding and attach the side stiles using the long screws. Finally, attach the top rail (E) to the upper edge of the headboard using the middle-sized screws.

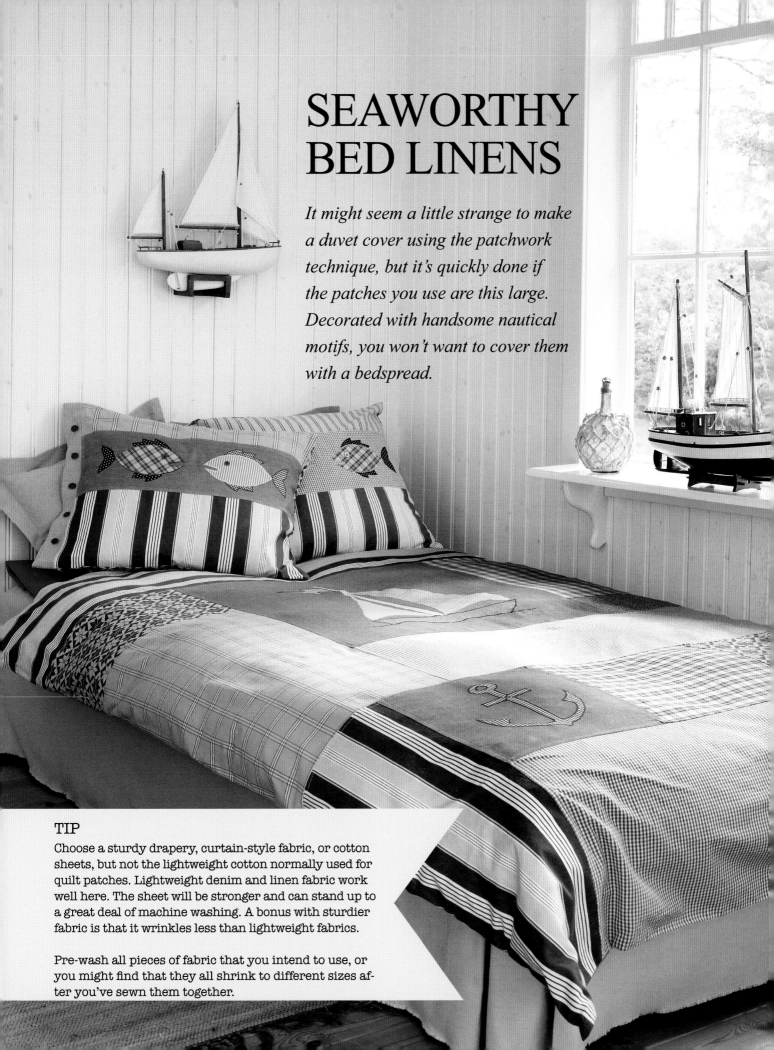

SEAWORTHY BED LINENS

It might seem a little strange to make a duvet cover using the patchwork technique, but it's quickly done if the patches you use are this large. Decorated with handsome nautical motifs, you won't want to cover them with a bedspread.

TIP

Choose a sturdy drapery, curtain-style fabric, or cotton sheets, but not the lightweight cotton normally used for quilt patches. Lightweight denim and linen fabric work well here. The sheet will be stronger and can stand up to a great deal of machine washing. A bonus with sturdier fabric is that it wrinkles less than lightweight fabrics.

Pre-wash all pieces of fabric that you intend to use, or you might find that they all shrink to different sizes after you've sewn them together.

PILLOW CASE & DUVET COVER

Hide that bedspread in the closet! When bed sheets are this pretty, it's quick and easy to make your bed by just shaking out the wrinkles and smoothing out the top. Using blue, white, red, and linen beige, mix leftover pieces with different patterns and maritime colors for a classic style with a salty taste of the ocean.

Add an extra touch! Decorate with appliqués of fine nautical motifs in different patterns. The duvet covers will feel exclusive and well made.

MATERIALS:

- Cotton and linen fabric
- Lining, 1 bottom/flat sheet
- Rivet buttons for jeans, 5 for each pillowcase
- Vliesofix appliqué back webbing
- Sewing thread

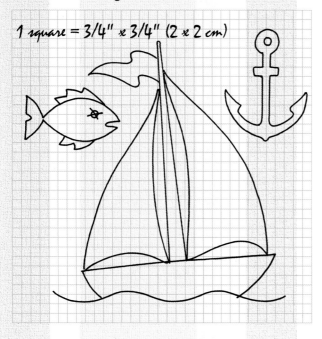

1 square = 3/4" x 3/4" (2 x 2 cm)

NAUTICAL MOTIFS

1. Use the diagram shown above, or draw a simple motif of your own design.
2. Vliesofix Fusible Paperbacked Web, or something similar, can be purchased by the yard in hobby or fabric stores. Place the Vliesofix over the diagram, glossy paper side up. Copy the different parts of the motif separately. The motif will be a mirror image of the diagram. Cut out the pieces roughly.

3. Set the iron thermostat to medium. With dry heat press the different motif pieces, glue the side toward the backside of the fabric (paper side up), for approximately five seconds. Let cool. Cut out the motif more precisely. Remove the protective sheet of paper. The glue is not sticky once cold.

4. Increase the iron thermostat to the cotton setting and use the steam function. Place the motif, glue side down, on the fabric being decorated. Press for eight to ten seconds to glue on the motif. Now you won't have to pin or baste the motifs, as they'll already be attached and stay put while you stitch a zigzag seam along the outlines. Use stitch length 0.8–1 and width 3.5–4, which will make a nice close seam that's decorative in itself. Choose a matching thread or a different one for a contrasting effect. The fish's eye is a sewn-on button, approximately ½"–⅝" (12–15 mm) in diameter.

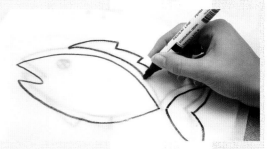

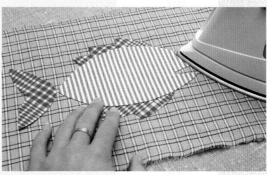

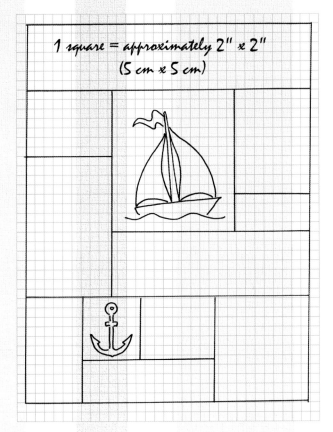

1 square = approximately 2" x 2" (5 cm x 5 cm)

HOW TO:

Seam allowance: Unless instructed otherwise, add ⅜" (1 cm) seam allowance to the pieces.

1. Use the diagram for inspiration and as a guide, but adjust the measurements to fit the amount and size of fabric you will work with. Use fewer but larger patches, or divide the diagram into smaller sections if you only use small leftover pieces. Don't forget to add a seam allowance of ⅜" (1 cm) along all edges on all pieces.

2. Stitch together all pieces with straight seams and zigzag or over lock the seam allowances. An extra chic touch is to press down the seam allowance and attach it with a decorative topstitch along the seam. Use a heavier linen-colored thread for this, and a stitch length of 4.

3. Once completed, a standard-size pillowcase patchwork piece should measure 20 ¾" x 26 ¾" (52 cm x 62 cm). The diagram for the duvet cover was made for a Swedish standard-size duvet and measures approximately 59" x 80" (150 cm x 203 cm) for the front of the duvet cover. By simply adding a 5" wide framing border around the patchwork, you will adjust it to fit an American twin-size duvet. Cut out the cover backing, preferably a prewashed flat sheet in a matching color, in the same size as the finished frontpiece.

4. **Quilted duvet cover:** Using a ½" (1 cm) seam allowance all around, stitch together the front and backing's long sides and top edges, right sides together. Then with a ¾" (2 cm) seam allowance, stitch together the bottom edges but leave a 23 ½" (60 cm) opening in the seam. Zigzag stitch or overlock the seam allowances. Along the seam opening on the sheet's bottom edge, fold the seam allowance double and stitch down a ⅜" (1 cm) wide hem. Turn the cover inside out.

5. **Pillowcase:** Stitch together the long sides and one short side. Zigzag stitch/overlock along the seam allowance.

6. **Button band:** Cut out a strip of fabric, 5" x 40 ¾" (12½ cm x 103 cm). Stitch the short ends together, right sides together, with a ⅝" (1½ cm) seam allowance. Press apart the seam allowance. Fold the strip double and lengthwise, wrong sides together.

7. On the right side, stitch on the button band around the pillowcase's open short side. Zigzag stitch/overlock the seam allowance. Press the seam allowance against the pillowcase fabric's wrong side and attach it with a decorative topstitch.

8. Make five buttonholes, each ⅞" (20 mm) long, evenly spaced along the button band on the front of the pillowcase. Rivet jeans buttons to the part of the button band attached to the back of the pillowcase.

SEA CHARTS & MAPS

Wanderlust, the thrill of exploration and adventure—fresh breezes drift in from the big world outside with the help of sea charts and maps. These are perfect materials when you can't wait to add something new and fresh to your surroundings.

PIRATE MAPS

Old maps and sea charts are amazing—on walls or still rolled up—but finding the real deal is neither cheap nor easy. We're in luck, however, because we can fake the age and patina with something most of us have at home—coffee. Start by ripping off a narrow strip of paper from all sides of a map to make them appear uneven. If you want it to look really used and old, dampen the paper by lightly spraying it on both sides with a spray bottle. Leave it to dry for about fifteen to twenty seconds. The dampness softens the paper, so you can carefully squeeze it lightly to wrinkle it. Smooth the paper flat again and let it dry. But even if you don't want to bother with wrinkling the paper, this next tip does the trick of giving it an instant patina. Set the paper down on a plastic surface and brush it with coffee. Let it dry. Once the paper is dry, iron it lightly with a cool iron.

LABEL LAVISHLY

Small labels are easy to make and are nice decorative accents to many bits and pieces. Attach small leftover bits of maps onto pieces of cardboard. A spray adhesive or a glue stick makes for quick and neat gluing. Punch a neat hole in the label with a hole-punch and attach a string or ribbon.

1.

2.

3.

YOU ARE HERE

4.

A COOL CLASSIC (see picture 1, p. 60)

Maybe you remember way back, when everyone wrapped textbooks for school in nice protective covers. (Does anyone still do that these days?) It's a great trick that works just as well for your own personal books, whether it is to protect them, to make a decorative stack for display, or to hide that novel you're ashamed to be seen reading in public. Use colorful maps and sea charts as wrapping and finish off by tying a coarse string and a nautical knot around a stack of them. It sets the style bang on!

PRETTY BOXES (see picture 2, p. 60)

You can turn nice lidded boxes and small bags from the hobby store into decorative storage once they have been covered in paper with pretty patterns. Even shoeboxes will do the trick.

The simplest way to do this is to use a few large glue sticks to apply adhesive directly on the object being wrapped instead of onto the paper. That way you avoid getting air bubbles in the paper and avoid an unsightly puckered surface. It also sets quickly.

WHERE IN THE WORLD? (See picture 3, p. 60)

Just in case you feel a little uncertain about where you are, it might be a good idea to mark your location squarely on a map. Glue a world map onto a porous display or a piece of foam board—basically, cardboard with a polystyrene center, which will allow you to stick pins in the board. To avoid any further confusion, I have also stamped the map with large letters in black acrylic paint. So now you also know that I can be found at the big red pin—in Sweden, to be precise.

EAST, WEST … SERVING TRAY
(see picture 4, p. 60)

Serve a cordial in Sicily and meringues in South America. A plain surface (a serving tray, for example) is spiffed up with the addition of a map. This works well for table tops, cupboard doors, and other flat surfaces, too. Glue the map onto the desired surface and give it a coat of clear water-based varnish for protection.

BUILDING BLOCK MAPS (see picture p. 61)

Building blocks to stack up high never lose their charm, even for adults. Ours are covered with maps and age-worn patina.

HOW TO:

The building blocks are made from a wooden post, 4" x 4" (100 x 100 mm), that is cut into 4" (100 mm) lengths to make square cubes. Sand the sawn surfaces and the sharp edges smooth. Cover all surfaces with maps by gluing them on with Mod Podge. To protect the maps' surfaces, add a topcoat of Mod Podge. Sand all the cubes' edges to remove some of the map print. Finish off the cube by sealing it with furniture wax in a warm brown tone—an oak color—to bring out a perfect patina. Tinted wax can be bought at most local paint dealers these days or even at furniture stores, as it´s often used to rebuff the wood surfaces.

PAPER WRAPPED FURNITURE

To renovate a piece of furniture by covering it with heavyweight paper is actually a far quicker job than painting it, as painting requires much more prep work, and the paint has to be carefully applied in several coats. However, it's tricky to fold and mold the paper properly around folds, corners, and edges. In other words, it's much smarter to paper only the flat, smooth surfaces. Prepare the piece of furniture's surfaces by cleaning and sanding them with fine grit sandpaper to achieve a matte finish. Wipe free of dust and clean. Paint the piece to be papered with a coat of primer. Then give all parts that are not going to be covered in paper, i.e. edges, corner, legs etc., two coats of interior paint of your personal choice. Make sure to also paint an inch or two in toward the surface to be papered.

How to paper:

Cut the paper to fit just a tiny, tiny bit smaller than the finished size. Brush it generously with wallpaper paste on the back of the map. Let the paper rest for about a minute or two to give it time to absorb the moisture and to swell in size ever so slightly. Place it against the surface to be papered and remove any air bubbles by brushing the surface with a wallpaper brush or a soft cloth if it's a small piece. Start brushing the paper from the middle and move outwards.

Let the item dry thoroughly, preferably for twenty-four hours. Once dry, protect the surface with clear, non-yellowing, water-based varnish to keep the white areas of the map white.

FURNITURE WITH A NAUTICAL FEEL

Scuffed, scratched, and dreary? Revive an old piece of furniture by dressing it in sea charts. The refreshed appearance of a chest of drawers also comes from the addition of new drawer handles made from coarse hemp rope. Drill two holes approximately 4" (10 cm) apart on the front of the drawer, and secure the handle by knotting the rope on the inside of the drawer.

LITERALLY

Take my word for it: make your own handsome letters papered with maps. Use wordplay by having the letters spell out something with a connection to the map. It could also be something simple such as ATLAS, MAP, WORLD, HOME, SEA, OCEAN, or why not the name of the place you call home?

Large letters for decorating is trendy, so visit your local craft store and search for letters with flat fronts in cardboard, wood, or MDF-board. Paint all over the letters with an acrylic paint. Then place the letter against the map and cut out the shape. Use a regular glue stick to attach the paper to the letter.

FASHIONED IN A FLASH

Sea charts are often printed on heavy-duty stock, which is perfect paper for cutting out pennants for a garland. They will not survive outside in hard wind or rain, but for an indoor nautical look it's hard to beat a sea chart for an inexpensive, easily assembled garland that looks great (see p. 65).

A SEASCAPE THAT LIGHTS UP

A smooth but boring lampshade can undergo a total makeover with the help of a sea chart.

Apply some Mod Podge on the back of the chart. Let the paper fill out for a few seconds and then wrap it around the lampshade. Smooth out any air bubbles. Once the lampshade is dry, paint a topcoat of Mod Podge evenly over the map and let it dry.

Once the sealant has dried, the paper will be completely stiff. This makes it easy to use an X-Acto knife and cut off the excess paper from the edge of the lampshade, which will give the shade a clean finish.

PS: The lamp base (see p. 65) is a thrift store find and was originally stained brown. Spruced up with some new color and soft, smooth pebbles from the beach, it has seamlessly joined the marine decor. The stones are glued on with a strong construction adhesive. Ask your local hardware store for advice on which brand to use.

SEAWORTHY ART

Decorative nautical wall art doesn't have to cost an arm and a leg. Check regularly at thrift and secondhand stores for deeply rimmed trays, small furniture drawers, even metal tins or wooden boxes, and anything that can be transformed into a shadow box (see p. 65). Paint a coat of primer if you need to and decorate the background with a sea chart. You don't need much more to finish it—a starfish, a beautiful shell or a stone wrapped in hemp string, attached to the edge of the shadow box. More common items found at gift and souvenir stores can become *objets d'art* if the shadow box acts as a presentation shelf to place the item on.

BUY MAPS . . .

- Sometimes common tourist maps detailing cities and provinces can be used for decor.
- Sea charts—found at ship chandlers in sea towns and on city waterfronts.
- Maps—scour thrift stores and secondhand bookstores for old atlases.
- Shop the Internet. Go surfing and you're sure to find web-shops that can offer all sorts of maps. Or take a shortcut and just hit www.amazon.com—they have plenty.

SHIP AHOY, WHAT A COOL LIFEBUOY!

Hopefully, you're not stranded in the water far from shore because these life preservers (also called "donuts") are completely useless if you need to be rescued in the water. They're purely decorative!

A STRAW WREATH IN DISGUISE

Can you buy life preservers at bargain prices at the florist? Of course you can! A plain straw wreath is a good starting point to make a life preserver with a more personal, handcrafted touch.

Any round, straw shape will work but the best ones are the ones used for floral arrangements at funerals because they are flatter and the straw is most compact and densely packed. Personalize it in your own chosen colors by wrapping the wreath with wide 1 ⅔"–2" (4 cm to 5 cm) strips of fabric. Red and white are not mandatory colors—play around until you hit the color combination that suits your taste and your home best. Wide cotton ribbons, burlap, or silver shining duct tape hold the rope in place around the life preserver. Fold the ribbon or fabric and stitch a seam (see diagram at right) to make a channel for the rope to slip through. Loop the ribbon or fabric around the life preserver and use a glue gun to fasten the ends to the back of the preserver.

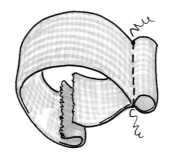

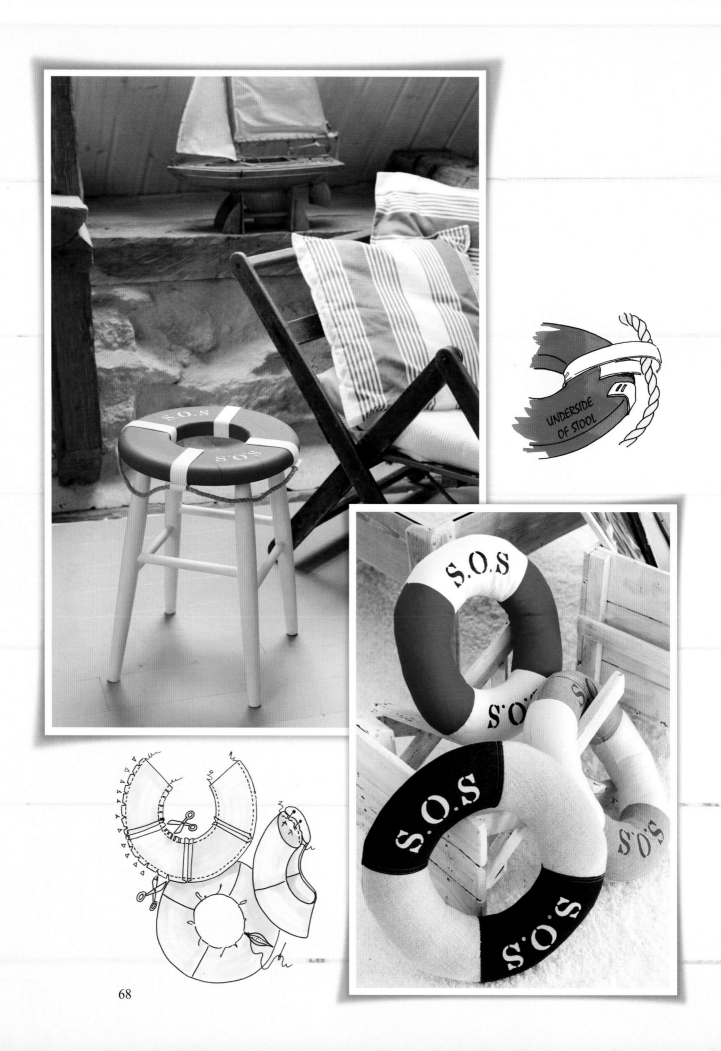

UNDERSIDE OF STOOL

68

REPURPOSED AS A LIFE PRESERVER

The thrift store was selling a totally generic wooden stool with a round seat. However, life took a turn for the better for this rather unremarkable object when it had its seat repurposed into a life preserver.

HOW TO:

1. Saw a round hole in the center of the stool seat, so it forms a wreath of approximately 4" (10 cm) wide. Sand over all sawn surfaces and smooth all sharp edges. Then sand the whole stool with fine sandpaper. Wipe off the dust and clean it with TSP or a similar product.
2. Prime the stool and paint the legs white and the seat red. Use a water-based acrylic paint for interior use. If you want to add the letters SOS to the preserver, make it easily by using stencils (see page 142).
3. Use a white, heavyweight canvas ribbon/band (the same type used for belts) and natural hemp rope (or the opposite colors—white cotton rope and linen beige ribbon/band). Fasten the band against the underside of the seat with a staple gun. Wrap the band around the seat, fold the other end around the rope, and fasten this end under the chair.

S.O.S.

Donut cushions will stop you from "sinking" too low into the couch.

Seam allowance: ⅜" (1 cm) is included in the pattern on the diagram.

MATERIALS:

Sturdy fabrics like cotton, denim or linen in two different colors. Pillow filler of choice. Heavy duty sewing thread.

HOW TO:

1. Using the diagram as a guide, draw the pattern in real size. Cut out eight pieces, four of each color.
2. If you want to add text to the donut cushion, use stencils and paint the text on the cut-out pieces before the cushion is stitched together. (To learn about how to use stencils, see p. 142.) Regular craft paint works just as well as textile paint for this project.
3. With right sides facing together, stitch four pieces (dark-light-dark-light) together along the short sides. Then place the two arc-shaped pieces right sides together and stitch both long, curved sides together. Make a second stitch right on top of the first seam to reinforce the seam.
4. Cut small V-shaped notches deep into the seam allowance along the outside of the donut without cutting the seam. Cut deep straight notches along the inner seam's allowance without cutting the seam. Turn the piece inside out.
5. Stitch the donut end openings, right sides together. It's a bit tricky to do this on the machine, but try to complete it a bit more than halfway.
6. Turn right side out and pack the donut as full as you can with your chosen filler. Close the donut ends by hand with a heavy-duty sewing thread.

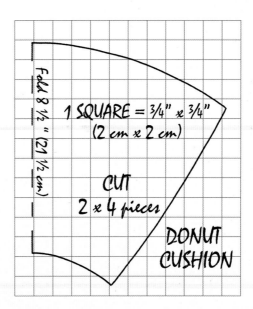

Fold 8 ½" (21 ½ cm)

1 SQUARE = ¾" x ¾" (2 cm x 2 cm)

CUT 2 x 4 pieces

DONUT CUSHION

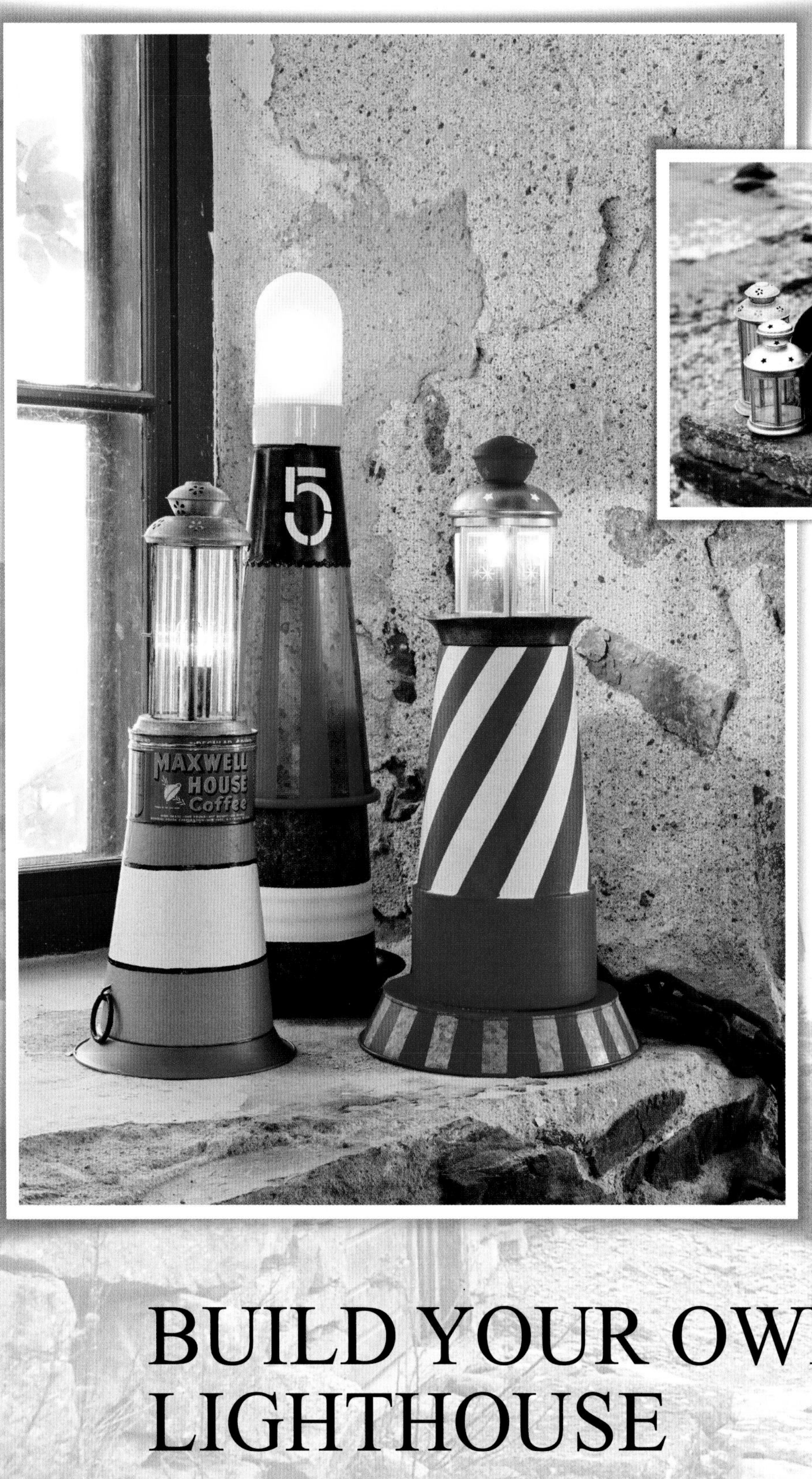
5
MAXWELL HOUSE Coffee

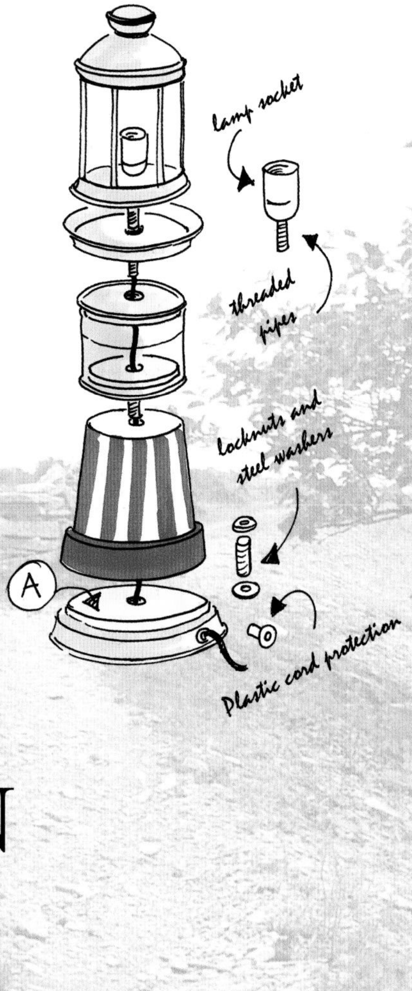
lamp socket
threaded pipes
Locknuts and steel washers
A
Plastic cord protection

BUILD YOUR OWN LIGHTHOUSE

Lighthouses are not only eye-catching landmarks, but they also light up our surroundings as well. Try your hand at building a lighthouse in the shape of a solid, large table lamp. You probably already have some of the required materials stashed away at home.

LIGHTHOUSE WORKSHOP

Most of us have pots and flowerpot saucers tucked away in storage somewhere. Perhaps some metal tins, a lantern, or a lamp can be scrounged up, too. If so, then you're well on your way. Pots, saucers, and tins are the building blocks that will create a lighthouse once they're pieced together. Turn the pieces upside down and sideways, stack them on top of each other, and build them up vertically. At the top is the very lantern room itself. The simplest way to create it is to use a lantern and a tea light, but you can also mount a proper electric light.

In order to paint the lighthouse, the pieces need to be made of metal, wood, or terracotta. Don't use glossy ceramics or porcelain here, as the paint will not stick. If you don't find many usable items in your home, see what you can find at thrift stores since they are generally full of the types of items you can use to build a lighthouse. Try stacking different things to see how they would look while you're still in the shop. This way, you'll have access to a vast assortment of bric-a-brac to try out.

OTHER MATERIALS:

- Acrylic paints from the craft store
- Metal primer
- Isopropyl alcohol
- Masking tape
- Plywood , ½" (12 mm) thick
- Silicone sealant, clear/transparent
- Sheet metal screw, flat head, size 8 x ½ (10 mm–15 mm)

FROM THE ELECTRICAL OR LIGHTING AISLE:

If you opt to bypass a lamp-ready kit, you'll need:
- Threaded pipes with corresponding locknuts
- Cord + plug + switch + protective plastic cord sleeve
- Light socket for small sized bulb

HOW TO:

1. Start by stacking and trying out several building blocks to find those that will make up the lighthouse. An upside-down saucer (metal/wood/terracotta) makes a good base for the lighthouse. Upturned pots and round metal tins add height. Many lighthouses have a ledge, or catwalk, around the light chamber itself. This can be made from a right-side-up saucer.

2. Add color to the lighthouse! Some pieces might already have a good tint, while others may need to be painted to give the impression of a working lighthouse. Metal surfaces will need to be sanded with steel wool or fine sandpaper to make the paint stick.

Clean off all surfaces with isopropyl alcohol. Protect all surfaces that are not to be painted with masking tape. Prime metal with a special metal primer before painting. After this prep work, feel free to use any acrylic paint (craft, hobby, or interior) you like. Terracotta pots and wood surfaces can be painted directly with acrylic paint from the craft store.

3. The easiest way to light up the lighthouse is to make a light chamber that requires only tea lights so that most of the lighthouse pieces can be glued together in one shot.

4. Pots glued to a flat surface need additional reinforcement, as the pot's edge is too narrow to have a strong grip. The solution is to saw a piece of plywood with a diameter only slightly smaller than the pot's inner diameter (see A on the diagram on p. 70). Check that the piece fits inside the pot. Attach the piece to the flat surface (a saucer perhaps?) with some glue. Reinforce it by fastening a screw from the inside of the saucer or tin to make the screw head keep the metal/terracotta in place.

5. If you want to mount an electric light and socket into the light chamber or install a complete lamp at the top, you'll need to make sure that all joints are sturdy and that the cord is protected so it won't be damaged. To do this, use threaded pipes with corresponding locknuts.
   - All thin metal surfaces need to be reinforced with plywood.
   - Predrill through-holes in all building blocks for the threaded pipes. The pipes are ⅜" in diameter, and the holes should be a snippet larger for easy assembling. If you want to use a regular lantern at the top, you must drill a hole through the bottom of the lantern, too.

6. Start the lighthouse from the top at the light chamber and build downwards. Mount the light socket on a threaded pipe and with a fair length of the cord, and place this in the light chamber. Secure it with locknuts. Proceed downwards and attach the different lighthouse building blocks with the bolts and locking nuts. Use glue where necessary. The cord follows each step and is threaded through.

7. When all the pieces are assembled, drill a hole on the side of the bottom plate large enough to allow the plastic protective sleeve for the cord to be pulled through. Attach the switch and plug. A suitable bulb is low wattage—preferably an LED light—small and pear-shaped.

BLUE, BLUE . . .

. . . wind and water? Well, blue jeans of course! This is recycling at its best. Old discarded denim clothing comes in a myriad of blue tones. The fabric is tough and hardly wrinkles, and has that loose, carefree attitude. With that kind of beachfront appeal, what could be more perfect to use in decorating details?

ROUGH AND READY FLAGS

The American and English flags look smart and decorative and are easily used as home décor. They are both easily recognizable when made with denim. The Swedish flag, unfortunately, is a very bright yellow and an intensely royal blue—very difficult to fit into trendy homes … So I tried to make an edgier version of a Swedish flag to honor my home country using blue jeans and beige linen.

The large cushion covers are made 16" x 20" (40 cm x 50 cm). A cushion inner pad of 16" x 24" will easily fit into the cover. The smaller cover measures approximately 12" x 16" (30 cm x 40 cm). You´ll be able to squeeze a 16" x 16" cushion inner pad into it. Use heavy-duty sewing thread. Seam allowances are pressed together (not open) toward one side of the seam. Make double topstitching along all the seams between the patches for a professional, clean finish.

American flag: From your stash of denim, cut three light pieces and four dark pieces of fabric, each measuring 3 ⅛" x 20 ¾" (8 cm x 52 cm). Using a ⅜" (1 cm) seam allowance, stitch the pieces together lengthwise to make a striped front piece. Using your darkest blue jeans, cut out a piece measuring about 7 ⅞" x 10" (20 cm x 25 cm). Fold in a ⅜" (1 cm) seam allowance along the bottom edge and the right short side. Press.

Place the square in the upper left-hand corner of the front piece and stitch it on with decorative topstitching. Paint one to three large white stars with textile paint on the dark-blue patch or attach a group of large star-shaped rivets (from your local crafts store).

English flag: Cut out a whole piece measuring 16 ¾" x 20 ¾" (42 cm x 52 cm) from a jeans leg. Use red and white striped fabric to cut out the strips for the flag's cross. It doesn't have to resemble the stripes on the English flag exactly, but it should be close enough so the flag is recognizable. Attach the strips with a close zigzag stitch along the cut edges.

Swedish flag: Cut a whole piece of denim measuring 12 ¾" x 16 ¾". Use natural-colored wide burlap ribbon or cut

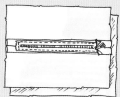

strips of linen. Stitch them on to make a cross.

In order to be able to wash the cushion covers, make inside covers. Cut out two pieces measuring 9 ⅜" x 20 ¾" (23 cm x 52 cm) for the larger sized pillow, and two pieces measuring 7 ⅜" x 16 ¾" (18 cm x 42 cm) for the smaller one. Using a 1" (2½ cm) seam allowance and placing the material with right sides together, stitch the long sides together, adding a 12" (30 cm) long zipper in the seam. Place the front and the back of the cushion cover with rights sides together. Stitch all around the outer edges. At the corners cut off the excess seam allowance. Edge the seam allowance with a zigzag stitch. Turn the cover inside out.

SAILOR'S BUCKET

Just like it sounds, this is a variation on a bucket. Early on, sailors used fabric buckets made of waxed sailcloth to bring much-needed water onboard. Make these "buckets" out of sturdy jean fabric. They turn into lovely beach totes stable enough to use as baskets.

Size: Large: 15 ¾" (40 cm) high and 13 ½" (34 cm) in diameter. Small: 12 ½" (32 cm) high and 11 ½" (29 cm) in diameter.

MATERIALS:

- Discarded jeans
- Heavy-duty sewing thread
- Expandable curtain wire or boning (used in fine clothing)
- Textile tape
- Sturdy rope, ⅝"–¾" (15–19 mm) diameter and just over 3 ¼' (1 m) long

HOW TO:

1. Cut up a pair of old jeans and use the patches to create a piece of fabric measuring 32 ¾" x 43 ⅝" (83 cm x 110 cm) for the large size and 26 ¼" x 37 ½" (67 cm x 95 cm) for the small size. Also cut two round circles for the bottom of the bucket measuring 14 ¾" (37 ½ cm) diameter for a large tote and 12 ¾" (32½ cm) in diameter for a smaller one.

2. Using a ⅝" (1 ½ cm) seam allowance, right sides together, stitch together the stitch short sides on the fabric you've created to form a cylinder. Press the seam allowances open. Fold the sewn cylinder, wrong sides together, to make a double-layered cylinder. Press along the folded top edge. Stitch a ¾" (2 cm) seam at the upper edge from the rim, but leave an opening of approximately 1 ½" (a few cm).

3. Take the curtain wire and cut off 45" (114 cm) for the large tote or 39" (99 cm) for the smaller tote. Thread the wire through the casing at the top of the tote. Join the spiral ends together, let them overlap by approximately 1" (2 ½ cm), and wind the ends together with textile tape.

4. Stitch four or five vertical casings from the top to the bottom edge, evenly distributed around the tote. For each casing, stitch two straight seams about ⅝" (1 ½ cm) apart. Cut off an equal number of lengths of curtain wire as you have casings, each 14 ½" (36 ½ cm) long for a large tote and 11 ¼" (28 ½ cm) long for a small tote. The ends of the spiral might be sharp, so wrap them in textile tape to protect the fabric. Insert the spirals into all the casings. Stitch a seam around the tote's lower edge ⅝" (1 ½ cm) in from the outer edge.

5. Remove a pair of belt loops from the waistband of a pair of jeans to use as attachments for the rope handles. Stitch the loops sideways, one on each side of the tote and just below the tote's upper casing. Turn the tote inside out.

6. Cut small, deep notches (without slicing through the seam) into the seam allowance at the tote's lower edge. Place the two bottom rounds together, wrong sides together. Pin and stitch the tote cylinder against the bottom circle—the tote's right side towards the bottom part. Use a zigzag stitch for the seam allowance and turn the tote right side out again.

7. Pull the rope through the side loops and tie two large knots at each end.

NEW LIFE FOR A SUN LOUNGER

Get the breezy ease of summer living all year-round by giving the sun lounger a place indoors. For a pittance it becomes a reading chair and looks cool and refreshed when the old canvas fabric is replaced with denim.

Use the old cover as a guide and pattern. Stitch together patches of denim from discarded jeans until you have one single piece that measures approximately 7 ¾" (20 cm) wider than the original fabric. Using extra heavy-duty sewing thread, stitch zigzag seams and press the seam allowance together in one direction. Stitch double decorative topstitching along all seams for extra strength. Fold and press a 2" (5 cm) wide, double hem along both long sides and topstitch them with double decorative seams. The wide hem adds firmness to the cover's shape. Attach the cover to the chair in the same way the original was attached.

TIP - Decorate with textile paint. Stripes can be taped directly to the fabric with masking tape. Stamps or stencils for letters and numbers can be found at the craft store.

THE QUICKEST DENIM CUSHIONS

By cutting out large sections and using the original fasteners from the denim shirts and skirts, making a cushion takes only ten minutes from start to finish. Spend a few more minutes and you can add a star for decoration, too.

The star appliqué is made in the same way as for the quilted duvet cover on page 57.

HOLD THE DOOR!

A leg from a pair of jeans makes a handsome and convenient doorstop. It works to block the door in an open position as well as to stop the door handle from hitting and denting the wall.

HOW TO'S:

Cut off a leg from a pair of jeans, about 14"–16" (35 cm–40 cm) up from the bottom hem. Stitch the leg together along the unhemmed opening. Fold out and stitch straight across the corners (see diagram). Turn the leg inside out, and you will have a small pouch. Place a plastic bag inside and fill it up with sand. Tie the plastic bag closed. Bunch the denim at the top and tie a knot with a sturdy rope around the opening.

QUICKLY MADE!

A pair of jeans can be scavenged and picked for parts in so many ways, down to the smallest detail. A tiny label or a loop can add just the right touch. I made the coolest lampshade out of leftover denim after I'd reserved the larger bits of fabric for other projects. And I didn't have to sew a single stitch! This lampshade can be made in less than half an hour, and the only tool required is glue. Set aside what can be saved from denim pants that you've already cut up. Rip the fabric to make shredded, torn edges; strip off labels and loops; and cut off the pockets. Using wallpaper paste or Mod Podge, coat both sides of the fabric generously with adhesive and attach the denim to the lampshade. The glue will completely dry the next day. If some pieces aren't quite stuck on (loops can be a bit challenging), just give them another hit with the glue gun.

You can make a simple lamp base very easily out of driftwood and old wood from a pallet. Start with a simple lamp base, such as a narrow pipe with a flat stand. There are lots of inexpensive ones at discount stores. Cut off the cord next to the electric plug. Turn the lampbase over and undo the locknut to remove the flat base from the pipe. Drill holes through the pieces of wood slightly larger in diameter than the pipe. Stack the wood pieces on the pipe. Reattach the flat base again, securing it with the locknut and attach a new electric plug on the cord.

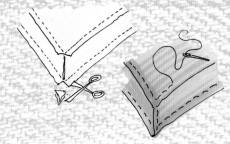

DURABLE SEATING

Whip up a slipcover for a polyester foam pad, and presto! A trunk or bench in the hallway becomes a welcoming place in your entryway.

HOW TO'S:

1. Order a 2"–3" (5 cm–7½ cm) thick polyester foam pad in your desired size from an upholstery business, or buy a cheap mattress at an outlet store. Use a carpet or X-Acto knife to cut it down to size.

2. The foam rubber surface tends to "catch," so you'll need to add a lightweight cotton lining first in order to remove the slipcover easily when you want to throw it in the laundry. The easiest way to do this is to wrap the pad in the lining material like a parcel and hand baste it in place with large stitches.

3. Stitch and join larger patches of the leftover denim pants to make larger pieces. Make the pieces 2" (5 cm) larger than the foam's width and thickness, and cut the top side in one piece. The bottom piece will be just as big but will be made from two pieces joined in the middle with a large opening in the seam.

OPENING

4. Cut and join pieces to form an edging strip 2" (5 cm) wider than the thickness of the foam and long enough to cover the pad completely. Stitch everything together with a ⅜" seam allowance and remove excess seam allowance in the corners. Turn the cover inside out. Press.

5. As you've probably realized by now, the cover material is too big; this is intentional so you can stitch decorative quilting seams along the edge of the pad. Do this by hand, and preferably with extra heavy-duty sewing thread. Grip around the seam

and make small basting stitches through all the layers of material, about ½"–⅝" (1–1½ cm) inside the seam. Do this along all seams on the pad and down the edging strip at each corner. This will bring the slipcover down to the right size, and that extra touch along the seams makes the result look great. Pull the cover over the foam pad and close the opening with large basting stitches. Glue Velcro onto the underside of the cover, and then glue the opposite band onto the trunk or bench to make the seating cover stay in place.

BLUE JEANS IN LATTICE WEAVE

Weave strips of denim together to make a nifty piece of work in many different shades of blue. It will look just as nice on the family couch as it will in a teenager's room.

DENIM CUSHION

Size: To fit inner pillow: 16" x 16" (40 cm x 40 cm)

MATERIALS:

- Scrapped jeans and jeans shirts
- Sturdy cotton fabric in denim blue, 1 front lining, 17 ½" x 17 ½" (45 x 45 cm), and 2 back pieces, 12" x 17 ½" (30 cm x 45 cm)
- 3 press studs, sturdy model
- Extra heavy-duty sewing thread

HOW TO:

1. Cut strips of denim fabric. Vary the width of the strips between 2 ½" (6 cm) and 3 ½" (8½ cm) and cut them at least 17 ½" (45 cm) in length.

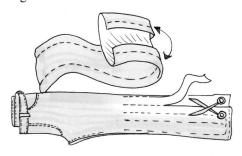

2. Fold in ⅝" (1 ½ cm) seam allowance, wrong sides together, along the strip. Press. Topstitch down the seam allowance with decorative seams along folded edges, stitch length 4. Use heavy-duty thread in contrasting color for best effect. For a rougher look, do not fold the seam allowances. Instead tear narrower strips measuring approximately 1 ¼"–2 ¼," (3–6 cm) and weave, leaving the raw edges visible.

3. **Blue cotton fabric/button band:** Do a zigzag stitch along one long side on both back pieces. Fold a 2" (5 cm) wide band towards the wrong side of the fabric. Press, and sew it down with decorative stitching. To add buttons, rivet press-studs along the button band —preferably sturdy studs that fit the style of jeans you're using. Rivet the buttons at 4" (10 cm) intervals. Snap the two back pieces together to make one whole piece.

4. Pin one end of the strips along one edge of the front lining. Mix up the strips—different shades and widths—for added appeal. Weave the strips in the other direction, shifting from over to under as you proceed. Here, too, mix the colors and widths. Pin the strips as you go to hold everything in place. When the latticed surface measures about 15¾" x 15¾" (40 cm x 40 cm), attach all the strips by sewing a straight seam all around just outside the lattice.

5. Pin the cushion cover's front and back pieces together, right sides together. Stitch a straight seam all around using a ⅝" seam allowance. Cut all the corners on the pillow to remove the excess seam allowance. Zigzag stitch the seam allowance. Turn the cushion cover right side out.

MATERIALS:

- Discarded jeans
- Cotton sheet for lining, 66" x 96" (167 x 243 cm)
- Zipper, 39" (100 cm), can be bought by the yard from a furniture upholstery supplier
- Regular sewing thread in denim blue
- Extra heavy-duty sewing thread
- 9 cubic foot bag (approximately 160 *l*) polystyrene beads. If you already have an old beanbag chair, reuse the old beads in your new chair.

TOOLS:

- Scissors
- Pins
- Sewing machine needle for denim jeans

HOW TO:

1. Draw the spool-shaped pattern pieces for the beanbag and for the lining bag according to the diagram in the following measurements (lining bag in red):

- **A** - height, 34 ¾" (88 cm) 43 ¼" (110 cm)
- **B** - upper edge, 3 ⅜" (8 ½ cm) 5 ½" (14 cm)
- **C** - 9" (23 cm) 16 ½" (42 cm)
- **D** - lower edge, 5 ½" (14 cm) 10" (25 cm) The bottom and upper part of the bag are shaped like two hexagons (six-sided),
- **E** - top, 5 ⅛" (13 cm), bottom, 9 ½" (24 cm)

2. Undo the crotch seams of the jeans you'll be working with. Cut along the inseam and lay the material flat so you can pin the spool-shaped pattern diagonally onto the jeans leg. Cut eleven "spools" of this piece in denim. Cut a twelfth spool, and cut that piece in half lengthwise and add a ¾" (2 cm) seam allowance along the middle (see diagram).

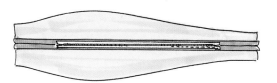

3. Sew the two halves together along the middle line using regular stitching at approximately 1 ½" (4 cm) at each end. Then machine-baste along the line where the zipper is to be set. Zigzag stitch the seam allowance and press it open. Hand-baste the zipper in place along the seam. Sew in the zipper using extra heavy-duty thread. Remove the machine-basted stitches.

A RETURN OF OLD FAVORITES

Dad's paint-splattered jeans, the kids' outgrown denim, your own out-of-date castoffs—old favorites can often get a new spark of life. Sew a large beanbag chair to sit in, and it's guaranteed to become an instant favorite! The bag itself has the shape of a large pear and is outfitted with a large zipper. A separate lining bag contains the filling, making it easy to remove the slipcover for laundering when needed.

Seam allowance: A ⅝" (1½ cm) seam allowance is included in all measurements.

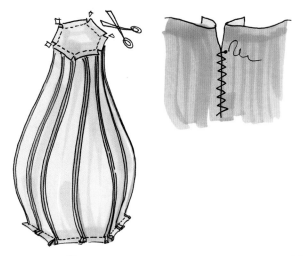
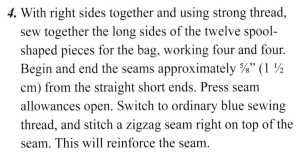

4. With right sides together and using strong thread, sew together the long sides of the twelve spool-shaped pieces for the bag, working four and four. Begin and end the seams approximately ⅝" (1 ½ cm) from the straight short ends. Press seam allowances open. Switch to ordinary blue sewing thread, and stitch a zigzag seam right on top of the seam. This will reinforce the seam.

5. Fun details! Remove back pockets, labels, and washing instructions from the jeans. Sew them onto the bag—this will definitely be noticed by the "label conscious" cool kids of all ages. Then sew together the last side seams so you have twelve attached pieces that make up a pear-shaped tube.

6. Sew the bag's upper edge around the hexagonal top piece; each second bag seam is pinned to a hexagonal corner. The bag's lower edge is sewn to the hexagonal bottom piece. Use extra heavy-duty thread for this. Notch a "V" in each corner of the hexagonal piece's seam allowance. Press the seam allowance to the wrong side of the hexagonal pieces, and sew it down along the hexagon's outer seam with a decorative topstitch using the extra heavy-duty thread.

7. Lining bag: You'll need to use good cotton sheeting for this (no flimsy lightweight crappy fabric). Sew it with heavy-duty thread to ensure strong seams that won't leak small plastic beads. Cut six spool-shaped pieces and one bottom piece. Sew together the long sides of the spool-shaped pieces. Then attach the lining bag's lower edge to the hexagonal bottom piece. Pour in the plastic beads through the upper opening. Fold down a seam allowance around the upper edge and sew the bag together straight across the upper edge. The lining bag should not be anywhere near full—the extra empty volume of the lining bag makes it malleable and easier to work the bag in and out of the opening of the jean coverslip.

ARTFUL MARKERS

Navigational buoys—or "markers" as they are also called—are very helpful to show the way when you're out boating. Of course, on land these are for decoration only, so if you decide to change the shape or color a little, they won't run anyone aground.

A MAKE-BELIEVE ARCHIPELAGO

A nautical navigational marker is a fun item, whether in the garden or on your own landing. But don't follow the herd! Glean inspiration from sea markers and warning buoys to make your own variations on the theme—a boat sign by the landing, a big float by your favorite spot for fishing, a fish in the garden where a dedicated fisherman lives…

OUTDOOR ARTY MARKERS

Paints: It doesn't require a lot of each color. If you have remnants from other outdoor painting projects, use them. Hobby stores also stock small bottles with special craft paints for outside use.

HOW TO:

1. You might be able to get some of the material for next to nothing. The thin wood strips—also called stickers—are commonly used for "stickering," or preventing wood boards from lying directly on top on one another when they're shipped in large batches to lumber yards or building stores. Usually those thin strips are discarded, so ask the salespeople to let you help yourself to a pile or two. They typically measure about 1 ⅜" (3½ cm) wide and approximately ⅜"–½" (8–10 mm) thick. The lengths may vary a little. They're not planed and have a rough surface, but that is easily fixed with a machine plane.

2. Place the strips of wood close together on a flat surface. Draw the middle line and the outline as shown on the diagram. Using a pencil, number all the strips according to placement. Use sandpaper to sand the sawn short ends smooth. Paint all the strips before you attach them.

3. You'll need a furring strip board, or if you prefer, weather-shielded lumber, measuring 2" x 2" (4 ½ cm x 4 ½ cm) thick and 8' (244 cm) long. If the marker is to be set in the ground, saw one end to a point.

4. It's easiest to paint the post separately. A furring strip board won't hold up as long outdoors, but is easier to paint. Weathershielded lumber might require special exterior oilstains. Ask your local paint supplier for advice.

5. Lay the post across a couple of sawhorses. As the post's sides are flat, all the strips can be set into their individual positions. You can mark with a pencil where the colors are to go on the post—the same colors as for the strips. The post is red where the red strips are to be attached, and white where the white strips are to be attached, and so forth. Paint the post.

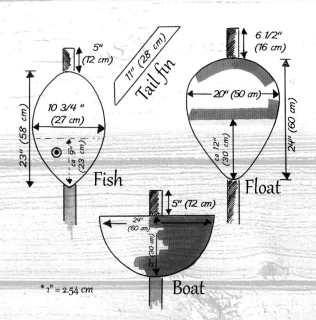

6. Place all strips next to each other on the post. Carefully lift every second strip of wood, press a dot of wood glue (for exterior use) directly onto the post, and place the strip back onto the dot of glue. Let dry. Remove the loose ribs and turn the post a quarter turn, and glue the rest of the strips at a 90° angle to the first set of strips. Once the strips are all attached, you can predrill and screw in all the strips. Predrill two holes, ⅛" (3 ½ mm) in diameter, into each strip. The holes are made diagonally to one another. Use self-tapping woodscrews.

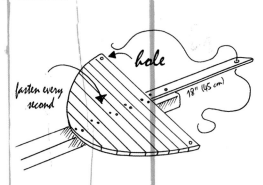

7. **Boat:** The mast is attached as an extension of the post. Drill a small hole at the top of the mast and at each outer end of the boat. Stretch a stainless metal thread or a string through the holes. To make pennants, cut a piece of cotton fabric measuring 2" x 5 ¼" (5 cm x 13 cm). For outdoor use, glue with shellac. Coat one side of the pennant entirely with shellac. Fold the fabric in two lengthwise around the metal thread or string. Let it dry. Brush some shellac on the outside of the pennant. Once dry, the pennant can be cut and its end trimmed to a point.

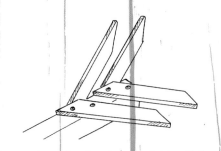

8. **Fish tail:** The strips forming the fish's tail fin are placed two by two on all four sides of the center post as shown in the diagram. Attach them with glue and screws like the other strips.

REMARKABLE INTERIOR MARKERS

Forget tchotchkes and small, fussy sea mementos! Make them large and impressive so they make a decorative statement in your home.

While you're at it, and since you already have the materials, make several of them. They make fine gifts that other sea and boat lovers will appreciate.

MATERIALS:

- Piece of wood for the base, measuring 5 ⅛" x 5 ⅛" (13 cm x 13 cm) and approximately ¾" (20 mm) thick
- Dowel, 21" to 22" (52 to 55 cm) long and ⅝" (15 mm) diameter
- Small, wooden, paint mixing sticks, approximately ⅝" (16 mm) wide, either from a paint store or from a shop selling them bundled as "kindling";
- Glue, glue gun
- Small wood screws, ½" to ⅝" (12 mm to 15 mm) long
- Drill bits, #46 (2 mm) and 4 1/64 in" (16 mm) diameter
- Sandpaper, medium grain

HOW TO:

1. Place the wooden sticks close together on a flat surface. Draw the midline and the outline of the marker. Using a pencil, number the strips according to their placement. Sand and clean off all sawn short ends. Sand the wood base and the dowel's upper end until soft and rounded.
2. Drill a hole in the middle of the wood base, 4 1/64 in" (16 mm) in diameter. Using a knife, sharpen the dowel's bottom end to a point. As the hole is slightly larger than the dowel, this will give the marker a slightly daring and rakish list.
3. Attach the small wood sticks quickly against the dowel with a glue gun. Start at about 1" (2 ½ cm) below the top of the dowel. Place the sticks closely together, every other one turned at a 90° angle. Once all the sticks are attached, predrill a small hole in each strip and secure it with a small screw.
4. Glue the dowel onto the wooden base plate. Paint the dowel with white craft paint in a flat finish. Once dry, block sections off with masking tape and fill in with a darker color. Real markers don't have the same striped "legs" that ours do, but as a decorative item it was much cheerier with many stripes, so I took some artistic license!

6" (15 cm)

10 1/2" (27 cm)

6" (15 cm)
Circle

1 3/4" (45 cm)

6" (15 cm)

87

"IF YOU LOVE BEING BY THE WATER . . . THEN IT'S NO WONDER YOU'LL WANT TO RECREATE THE SAME FEELING AND ATMOSPHERE IN YOUR HOME."

BEACHCOMBING

A beautiful pebble as smooth as silk; a soft branch, gray, twisted, and weather-beaten; a fine-looking shell . . . Treasures have many faces, and discovering them is one of the pleasures of beachcombing along the shore, head bent and eyes riveted to the ground.

AN EASEL FROM THE BEACH

Display a small painting or picture by setting it on a table easel made from driftwood and soft sticks. If you can't collect enough raw materials from the beach, you can fudge things a bit by getting some dry sticks from a wooded area. When sticks have been lying around for a long time, their bark disintegrates. They are smoothed over by the weather and the wind . . . and eventually end up looking very much like driftwood.

A DRIFTWOOD MINI GARLAND

They don't look like much, do they? Those small pieces of driftwood found on the beach. Can a pile of twigs be turned into something unique or interesting? Sure! A number of small pieces can be strung onto a piece of string to make a fine garland.

If you drill a hole in the center of the wood, the garland will look neat but maybe a bit boring. But if you set your pieces a bit off-center and slightly in from one of the edges, you suddenly have a sprawling garland that sways and twists gently in the breeze. Don't overthink how the pieces should be placed. Just string them on, tie a knot between each piece, and let them land where they may. It will come out just fine without too much pre-planning.

BRING A BIT OF THE BEACH HOME!

Build a coffee table to showcase your very own bit of beach. To achieve that authentic feel of weathered driftwood, I used wood from an old pallet and pallet collar that had turned gray after being left outside in the elements. The tall pallet collar makes it a box on legs where there's room for sand, pebbles, driftwood, a skein of hemp rope, and other unique beachcombing finds.

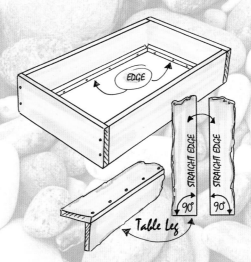

MATERIALS:

- 1 pallet collar, 8" x 31 ½" x 47 ¼" (200 x 800 x 1200 mm)
- 1 loading pallet
- 1 board of plywood for the bottom part
- Furring strips measuring 1" x 1" (25 x 25 mm)
- Wood glue
- Screw with a flat head, 1 ⅜" and 1 ½" (35 mm and 40 mm) long
- Glass for the table top

FOR VISIBLE MOUNT:

- Use slotted screws with round heads, preferably brass, and measuring 1 ½" (40 mm) long

HOW TO:

1. Start by sawing the pallet apart and cutting the longest pieces possible. These will be used for the table's legs, so the board length will equal the height of the table. Saw off the metal corners on the pallet collar. If the wood has been taken in from outdoors, let it cure (dry) for a couple of weeks.

2. The pallet collar is 8" (200 mm) wide, which will be the height of the box itself. You can change width and length of the table according to your own preferences. Cut the pallet collar wood into four pieces to fit the table's width and length.

3. *Box:* The furring strips will become the edge that supports the bottom board. Cut the strips into lengths as you did with the pallet collar, but make them 4" (10 cm) shorter. Glue and screw in the strip edging along one long side of each board, starting 2" (5 cm) in from the short end. Use a flathead screw for this. Sand the boards smooth. Glue and screw together the box frame.

4. *Legs:* You'll need two pallet boards for each leg. One long side is straight while one short side is cut at a 90° angle to the straight side. You can saw the other long and short side, however, as rough and weird as you please. Perhaps you want to whittle it a little with a knife to make the piece look more like driftwood. Then sand and polish the wood. (Read more about how to make driftwood from a loading pallet on page 39.)

5. Glue and screw the boards together, two and two, at a 90° angle, straight sides together. Brass screws tend to be rather soft and their heads can be easily damaged by the screwdriver so use care and make sure to pre-drill holes wherever you want to add a screw. Five screws, evenly spaced, should do the trick.

6. The legs should go over the box's upper rim by a minimum of ⅜" (1 cm) in order to keep the glass plate in place. Using a pencil, measure and mark the position of the lower edge of the box frame on the inside of the legs. Glue the legs in place. Once the glue has dried, reinforce the legs with four to six brass screws in each corner to make the tabletop box stay in place.

7. Measure the inside width and length to cut the bottom board. Screw it in place. Caulk the plane's outer edges with latex sealant to stop any sand from leaking.

8. Measure the surface of the tabletop and order a sheet of glass ¼" (6 mm) thick with polished edges. The legs protect the corners of the glass and keep the sheet in place. Fill the table with dry sand and beachcombing treasures.

THE RETURN OF THE BOTTLE LAMP

It's time to revive an old friend by making a lamp out of a really big bottle or a small glass vessel known as a carboy or a demi-john. Scour thrift stores for suitable items. Clear or slightly green-tinted glass will look great when filled with beautiful pebbles or sand from the dune at your favorite beach. Home Depot sells a kit with a lamp harp and socket attached to a stabilizing plug that's inserted into the bottle opening. If the bottle opening is too wide, increase the width of the plug by winding it with white textile tape.

The lampshade is a basket from which the handles have been snipped off. Its support is the metal frame of an old, disused shade. The text is stenciled on with spray paint. (To read more about how to use stencils, see page 142.)

SHOWCASE FOR SHELLS

Collect your treasures in large glass jars or under glass domes, and leave them around as eye candy. That way you'll have ONE impressive ornament instead of many little trinkets. And there will be less dust. Can you beat that?

BEACH MEMORIES

Sand from your island vacation, a beautiful feather, smooth pebbles . . . Ordinary glass canning jars make attractive containers for both a handful of beach mementos and a photograph. Canned memories warm our souls so well in the gloom of dark winters.

94

WHIMSICAL CHANDELIER

Downplay the elegance and take the edge off the romance by adding a pair of scraggly starfish to a crystal chandelier. Wind a string around one of the starfish's arms and hang it with a casual knot, leaving the ends dangling.

THE MORE THE MERRIER

Sometimes it's the sheer number of things that makes it look so charming. Pour it on and cover a wreath with a random bunch of starfish. And not one living starfish was harmed in this project, as they are all made out of clay!

CLAY STARFISH

Use any kind of clay or modeling material from the craft store that appeals to you. Some can be air-dried while others need to be dried in your kitchen oven.

Make a ball out of the clay (1) and then flatten it slightly. Nip and tuck to mark out the five "arms" (2). Gradually shape, press, and mold the ball of clay with your fingers until you end up with five slim "arms" (3). Starfish all look different and come in different sizes—that's part of their charm. On the starfish's underside, with a wooden stick, make a line so you have an indentation lengthwise on each arm (4). Then to mark the upper side and give it texture, prick it lightly all over with the blunt end of a stick.

The arms of the starfish might be too fragile and difficult to drill through, so try winding some natural string around the end of an arm to attach it to the chandelier.

SEA WIND CHIMES

You won't find any exotic shells on the beaches around my neighborhood — and no starfish either for that matter. We'll just have to accept this state of affairs and buy those items in a craft store or at www.etsy.com (search for "capiz shell discs"). What's really great about the big, white, almost translucent capiz shells (mother-of-pearl discs) is their sound—their gentle jingle and tinkle. They're just perfect for making a wind chime! Flesh that idea out some more, and they soon become chimes, decorative garlands, and a privacy screen all in one!

HOW TO:

1. Begin with a coarse hemp rope. Use a thinner rope and make two loops to use for hanging. Glue the loops to each end of the hemp rope with a glue gun and wind some natural twine around them tightly. It should be wound approximately 1" (a few cm) wide—not just to secure the loops but also as an added decorative detail.

2. Use a thin, natural twine to hang seashells and starfish. You can drill holes in the shells, but since they might be hard, use a drill for metals. You can also make it easier on yourself by folding the twine in half, and gluing the folded end with a drop of superglue to the inside of the shell. To add a nice glint, mix in some crystals or glass prisms. Hang the items at different heights. The closer together you tie the objects, the more variation in height you can have. The garland in the picture is approximately 8"–10" (20 cm–25 cm) in height. If the decorations are tied closer together, some of it can be strung up with really long pieces of twine, at which point the height of the garland could easily reach 12" (30 cm).

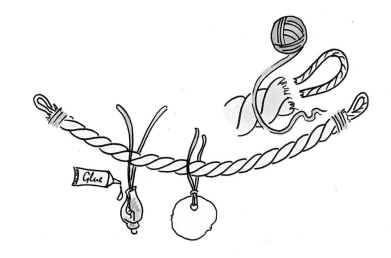

ROLLING BLUE WAVES

Recycled button-down shirts are wonderful to remake into patchwork quilts. Squares, stripes, and dots in different shades of blue are reminiscent of gleaming water and rolling blue waves. Fresh, clean, and exquisite for summer!

"... THE INTERIOR DECOR TAKES ITS CUES FROM THE BEACH AND THE FANTASTIC AQUATIC LIFE IN AND AROUND THE SEA ..."

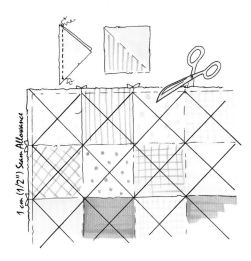

THE BIG BLUE

Collect piles of discarded blue/white cotton shirts and use them for patchwork. Mix a variety of patterns and blues; they don't have to match perfectly to make a beautiful ensemble—quite the opposite, in fact. Perfection can be plain old boring.

A PATCHWORK QUILT

No, we're too lazy to hand quilt and too eager to have this ready for use! The challenging part in making patchwork quilts all by machine is handling the large quantities of fabric while sewing. To remedy this problem, you can sew the quilt in smaller sections and then finish the quilt by stitching the already quilted sections together.

Size: 44" x 69" (112 x 175 cm)

Seam allowance: ⅜" (1 cm) seam allowance is included in all measurements.

Patches: 80 patches/squares of shirt/lightweight cotton fabric, each measuring 8" x 8" (20 cm x 20 cm)

Lining/patchwork backing: 4 pieces, 17 ⅜" x 42" (44 cm x 107)

Batting: 4 pieces quilt batting, 16 ½" x 41 ¼" (42 cm x 105)

Border frame:

A - 2 strips of the lining/backing material, 3 ½" x 42 ¼" (9 x 107 cm)

B - 3 ½" x 70 ⅛" (9 x 178 cm)

Shadow edging: Cut a 4 ¾" (12 cm) wide strip in the same amount and lengths as the edging/binding strips.

Seam allowance binding: If it will be "invisible," same as the lining/backing material. If it will be decorative detail, use shirt fabric: 4 strips, 2 ⅜" x 42" (6 cm x 107 cm).

HOW TO:

1. Place all the cut patches on a flat surface, i.e. 8 x 10. Place the patches into a unique layout. You might have just two or three patches of some fabrics/prints, and from other fabrics/prints there might be seven, eight, or more, so it takes some planning to match them nicely in an overall combination. Stitch together all the patches, first in long rows and then stitch the rows together to form the full patchwork quilt section. Press the seam allowances open after stitching each seam.

2. Draw diagonal lines in both directions across the quilt. Remember that the ⅜" (1 cm) seam allowance around the quilt is not to be included, so the diagonal lines will meet/end ⅜" (1 cm) inside the cut outer edge. Cut all patches along the drawn lines. There will be a lot of "extra" triangle patches along the edges, but you'll need those, too. Sew them together two by two to form complete square patches. Press the seam allowances open.

3. There are now a total of 160 bicolored patches measuring 4 ⅛" x 4 ⅛" (10 ½ cm x 10 ½ cm). Now repeat Step 1. Place all patches on a big flat surface. You'll have 16 rows with 10 patches in each row. Move them around and find a layout that pleases you.

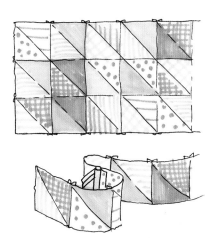

4. Sew together the patches in each row, ten patches in each strip. Press all seam allowances open. Then stitch together four strips to make a larger piece of 4 x 10 bi colored patches.. Press the seam allowances open.

USEFUL INFO ABOUT FABRIC

- All fabrics—for patches as well as lining—must be prewashed before being cut and sewn. If not, the pieces might shrink unevenly the first time you wash the quilt in the laundry.

- Batting is easier to work with if it isn't excessively fluffy. Craft and fabric stores sell specialty batting for quilts. Fleece blankets work well, too, and can be an option for batting.

- The quilt backing/lining can be made from sturdier fabric than the lightweight fabric patches. My quilt is lined with a natural beige linen fabric. The coarse weave and the sandy color make a nice contrast to the shirt fabric's blue shades. Lightweight denim would also look nice, but it's seldom sold by the yard. However, you may find this fabric sold as curtain panels or sheets, so keep your eyes open for them!

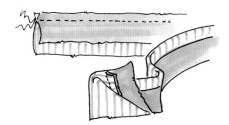

5. Place a piece of lining material on a flat surface, wrong side up. Center the batting on the lining and set the patchwork piece on top, wrong side facing the batting. Baste together the pieces along the outer edges. Then baste through all layers back and forth across the surface to keep all the layers in place. Basting is no fun, I'll grant you that, but it does make it easier to quilt nicely and you avoid sticking your fingers with the pins or having them slip out of place. Use stitches 1 ⅛"–1 ½" (3–4 cm) in length to make the basting go a bit faster. Use a long, slim sewing needle and extra heavy-duty thread. Machine stitch a zigzag seam along the piece's outer edge.

6. *Quilting the patchwork:* Set the sewing machine on stitch length 4 and change the thread to extra heavy-duty thread for quilting with decorative topstitches. Sew along the seams between the different patches—not right on the seams themselves, but parallel to the seam and slighty (a few millimeters) to the side. You don't have to stitch along all the seams between the patches to get the patchwork to actually hold together, but the end result will look so much nicer if you take the time and have the patience to do it. The more seams there are, the prettier the quilt. That's a fact.

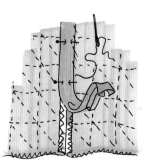

7. Stitch together the four quilted sections along the long sides to make it all one big quilt. Press the seam allowances open. They will show on the back of the quilt, and that's where you'll use the seam allowance binding. Pin the binding on top of the visible seam allowance. Using whipstitch, attach the binding along the long sides by hand.

8. *Border frame:* With right sides together, sew strips together for border and shadow edge along one of the long sides. Fold up and press the seam allowances against the wrong side of the border fabric. With wrong sides together, fold border and shadow edge over lengthwise. Press.

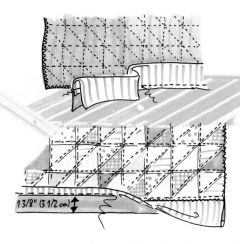

1 3/8" (3 1/2 cm)

9. Start with the shortest (**A**) strips for the border frame. With the front of the border fabric turned towards the back side of the quilt, stitch the border strip along the quilt's short side. Fold down the border and press the seam allowance over on to the border strip. Turn the quilt over to the other side and fold the border strip double lengthwise so it covers the seam allowance right. Pin it down on the right side of the quilt. The border is folded so that the border fabric measures to a width of 1 ⅜" (3½ cm), shown as beige here on the illustration, while the striped shadow edging will be a ⅜" wide edge. Attach the border with a decorative topstitch along the seam between the striped shadow edge and beige border frame. Thanks to the many layers of fabric in the border frame, the framing is nicely firm without any extra padding with quilt batting.

10. To edge the quilt's long sides, first fold in ⅜" (1 ½ cm) seam allowance along the binding's short sides, wrong sides together. Press. Repeat the procedure in Step 9.

MIXED & MATCHED

Do you have some leftover fabric from the shirts? Perhaps there's enough to make matching cushions. The smaller cushion uses the same technique as the patchwork quilt.

But even the smallest pieces can be used! They'll add fun to a cushion as a row of cheery pennants. The look is more intricate on a cushion of unbleached linen fabric with a beautiful texture than on ordinary white cotton fabric.

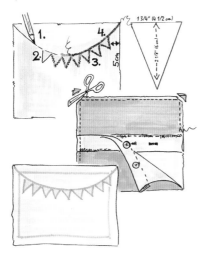

MATERIALS:

Cushion fabric, a sample of lightweight cotton fabrics; Vliesofix Fusible Paperbacked Web (or similar); three buttons, approximately ¾" (20 mm) in diameter

HOW TO:

1. Measure your cushion inner pad. Add 4" (10 cm) to the width and length for the front of the pillow, and cut out the piece in your chosen fabric for the cushion cover. Cut two back pieces. The width of the back piece should equal half the width of the front + 3" (7½ cm), and the back's length should be the same as the front's length.

2. Draw a sweeping curve going from corner to corner. Iron on fusible fleece on the wrong side of the shirt fabrics. Cut out the pennants and place them along the curved pencil line. The fusible fleece on the fabric's wrong side acts as glue, and the pennants will stick to the cushion front when you iron them. Program the sewing machine to a close zigzag stitch, 0.8–1, and a stitch width of 4–4 ½. Sew only along the outside of the pennants. When all the pennants are attached, stitch along all the pennants' upper edges, as one continuous zigzag seam all along the curved line.

3. Button band: Zigzag stitch along one of the back's long edges. Fold down a 2" (5 cm) wide hem, wrong sides together. Press and stitch down. Make three buttonholes along the button band, each approximately ¹⁄₁₆–⅛" (2 mm) longer than the diameter of the button. Repeat on the second back piece, except add buttons to the button band instead of buttonholes.

4. With right sides together, sew the cushion pieces together. Using a ¾" (2 cm) seam allowance, sew the cushion's outer edges together. Cut off the corner excess seam allowance at a bias. Turn the cushion inside out. Press.

5. Topstitch a decorative seam all around the cushion cover. This seam will show off nicely if also done with a close zigzag stitch, 1 ⅛" (3 cm) in from the outer edges.

VANITY CARPENTRY

Stash your quilts on a shelf and stuff the sofa throws in a basket? Anyone can do that! So why build a wooden stand? Well, to make a real show of your nicest textiles. It looks nice and adds a cozy touch.

QUICK AND EASY WOODWORK

You can use the stand as a drying rack, a high-boy, or as a display rack for quilts, plaid blankets, or other textiles set out for decoration. I've made this stand extra wide, but you can choose to make yours more modern—a bit more like a step ladder. Especially if using it for towels in a bathroom, where space might be tighter.

WOOD FRAME

47" (120 cm) wide, 71" (180 cm) tall, 23 ½" (60 cm) deep

MATERIALS:

- Pine boards; 4 pieces in common size, 1" x 3" (the actual size is a little less), length 73" (21 mm x 70 mm x 1850 mm)
- Furring strips, common size 1" x 2" (again, the actual size will be smaller) (25 mm x 50 mm)
  - 2 pieces: 48" (122 cm)
  - 2 pieces: 43 ¼" (110 cm)
  - 2 pieces: 38 ½" (98 cm)
- Dowel: 1" (25 mm) in diameter, 46 ½" (118 cm)
- Dowel: ⅜" (9½ mm) diameter; 2 pieces measuring 2" (5 cm) long
- Chain, 2 pieces measuring 16" (40 cm)
- Screws with big flat head, approximately ¾" (20 mm) long to fasten the chain
- Wooden screws, preferably with round head, #10, length 2" (50 mm)
- Drill bits, #18 (4 mm), ⅜" (9½ mm), 1 ⁵/₆₄" (27 mm)
- Sandpaper
- Stain and brushes

TOOLS

- Saw
- Jigsaw
- Power drill
- Planer (machine)
- Tension strap

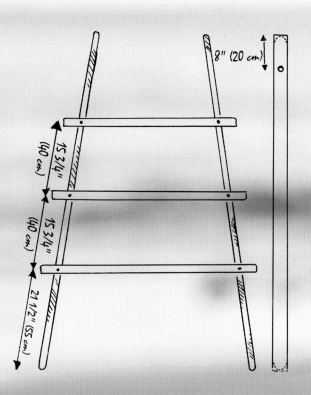

105

HOW TO:

1. Drill holes for the dowel in all four boards, 8" (20 cm) in on one of the short ends. The hole is drilled 1 $^{5}/_{64}$" (27 mm) in diameter, deliberately larger than the dowel's diameter. Saw all board ends into a rounded shape. Plane and sand all frame pieces smooth, and round all sharp edges and corners.

2. It's simplest to paint all pieces before assembling the frame. Use any type of paint you like, but it's nice to use a glaze or stain that allows the wood grain to show through.

3. On all furring strips, drill a centered pilot hole, 4" (10 cm) in from each short end, using drill bit size #18. Place the four pine boards on their short sides, side by side, and drill pilot holes at the distances shown on the diagram.

21 1/2" (50 cm) *15 3/4 (40 cm)* *15 3/4 (40 cm)* *15 3/4 (40 cm)*

4. Screw on the furring strips to make two ladders. So far the construction will feel pretty unstable. Place the two "ladders" together, back against back, with the side boards parallel. Push the dowel in through the top end holes.

5. Place a strong tension strap around the frame just under the dowel and tighten the strap hard. As the holes are larger than the dowel, the sides can be pulled in and bent into a slight bow-shape. This adds tension to the frame and makes it more stable. When you can't tighten the strap any further, mark the dowel for a wedge pinhole on each outer side of the frame.

6. Loosen the tension strap just enough so you can remove the dowel and drill the two wedge pinholes through it, $^{3}/_{8}$" (9½ mm) in diameter. Sand the pins (small pieces of dowel) and whittle one end with a knife to a sharp point.

7. Return the dowel to the frame, tighten the tension strap again, and knock the wedge pins into place. Remove the tension strap.

8. Screw the chains to the outside of the frame's sides, one on each side of the frame at the same height as the lower step. The chain will prevent the ladder from sliding apart and helps to stabilize it.

ROPE TRICKS

A neat five-minute trick for decorating with a maritime atmosphere is to hang a skein of sturdy hemp rope or lines on a wall hook, or throw a few bundles of rope in a basket. If you feel a bit more ambitious, using rope is still a good way to refresh old things. Old and worn items can be covered in the blink of an eye and be both beautiful and nautical.

BEACHFRONT HEADBOARD

You don't need to be a master carpenter to put together a good-looking headboard for your bed. The charm and beauty in this rough-hewn headboard is in its simplicity.

HOW TO:

1. Tongue and groove boards from a building supply store will work, of course, but nearly any kind of board will fit the bill here. It doesn't matter if they're different widths. In fact, it could make the headboard look even more charming. The boards can even vary a little in thickness, but only by a few fractions of an inch. I used leftover scrap lumber in different widths and cut them all down to 47" (120 cm) lengths.

2. Beware! Rough and splintery wood holds no charm, especially when used in a headboard. Collect enough boards to get the width of the headboard you want, and cut the end of the boards straight across. If you use tongue and groove boards, saw off the tongue and groove on the two outer boards to get flat edges along the sides of the headboard. Sand the board surfaces first with medium coarse and then fine sandpaper. By all means, let the boards have texture, visible veining, and flaking paint, but make sure to finish their surfaces so they feel smooth to the touch. You don't want a dust collecting headboard that can't be wiped dust free!

3. To achieve right angles, work on the floor and use the corners of the room as your guide. Place the boards, backs up, and push them together so they fit snugly against both walls in the corner. Attach two rails straight across with screws to hold the boards in place. If the upper rail is a wood molding that can be used upside down as well to interlock two moldings, the board can be easily hung on the wall when ready. Add a few furniture sliders along the joint. When ready to hang, fasten another wood molding on the wall, facing upward.

4. Round off the headboard's upper corners. Use an ordinary saucer or plate as a guide and draw a half circle to round the corners. Saw with a jigsaw.

5. Attach a hawser (a very sturdy rope) along the headboard's edge. The hawser ends are wound with natural twine, both to hold the strands together and to provide a decorative element. Quickly attach the hawser to the headboard with a glue gun to keep it in place. Then reinforce it by nailing it down; long, slim brads disappear into the hawser and become almost invisible.

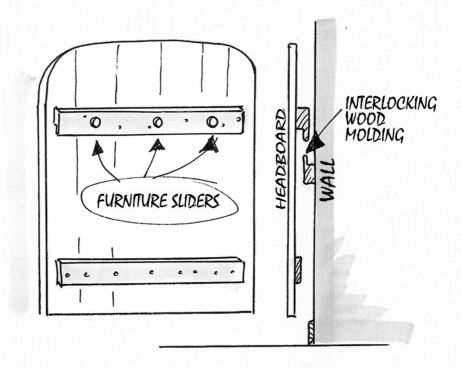

FURNITURE SLIDERS

INTERLOCKING WOOD MOLDING

HEADBOARD

WALL

QUICK MIRROR RESTORATION

A plain framed mirror from a thrift store and a bundle of rope creates a stylish mirror in no time at all!

Plain, homely, and the duller the frame, the better—as long as it's round or oval in shape. You don't have to paint it, as the rope will cover the entire surface. But do give it a good sanding with coarse sandpaper to allow the adhesive to grip better. Wipe the frame clean with denatured alcohol.

One row of hawser rope will have a very nice effect. Bind the edges with natural twine, both to hold the strands in place and for a decorative touch. Use a glue gun to attach the rope and carefully nail in a few brads to secure it all. On each side of the coarse rope, attach hemp rope with your glue gun.

A COARSE, LOOSE WEAVE

You can make awesome curtains for mere pennies from cheap burlap.. When they've done their time in your windows, they can be recycled and put to other uses around your house. The loose burlap weave can be ironed flat or soaked and scrunched up tightly and left to dry in a wrinkled heap. A few wrinkles look a bit silly, but when the fabric is completely creased, it becomes a fun decorative detail. Use hawser rope as tiebacks. Add a loop at each end. (For the shell garland, see page 97.)

BALANCING SIDE TABLE

Trick the eye a little! Make a table that at first glance looks like it's balancing atop rope legs.

The "bones" for the legs can be found at building supply stores, thin, slim metal pipes with a simple foot screwed to the tabletop's underside. Choose metal legs as small as possible in diameter to make the rope trick as convincing as possible, preferably around 1 ¼" or even less. The legs come in different lengths so they can be adjusted to your project.

What about the tabletop? Search thrift stores with an open mind and look for anything at all that will work as a tabletop. The shabbier the better—an old door, an old garden bench. Scrub it down and sand it.

To make it look as if the table is resting on rope, make big knots out of coarse rope, ⅞"–1" (20 mm–25 mm) in diameter, to be fastened onto the tabletop. One end of the knot will show, but the other must disappear down into the tabletop, so drill large holes for the rope over the placement of the four legs.

Turn the tabletop upside down and screw in the metal legs. Use hemp rope, ¼" (6 mm) in diameter. Fasten the end of the rope to the underside of the tabletop with a staple gun. Wind the rope tightly around the leg. To make the rope stick tightly to the end of the leg, tape a few rows around the leg first with duct tape. You can now glue the rope on with an ordinary glue gun or use a stronger glue with longer drying time.

MAGICAL ROPE LAMP

Yes, it is a bit tricky to make a lamp stand that looks like a floating rope, but it is still not as difficult as the real magic rope trick. And it is rather nice to be able to boast that you've made this awesome lamp yourself!

MATERIALS:

- Flexible copper piping ½" (12 mm) diameter
- Hemp rope, ¼" diameter
- Natural color hemp twine
- Lamp cord + switch + plug
- Screw-thread lamp socket with screw-in-fitting for lampshade
- Threaded pipe, ⅜" (10 mm) diameter, found in the electric or lighting aisle
- Drill bit, 3 ¹⁄₆₄" (12 mm) diameter + power drill
- Duct tape
- Glue gun
- Superglue
- Super strong construction adhesive (at your local hardware or building supplier)
- To make the lamp base, a large stone and drift-wood, or a piece of slightly rough-looking wood.

HOW TO:

1. It's important to buy the right kind of pipe! It has to be flexible copper piping that can be easily bent and warped. To start with, cut the pipe to the right length, approximately 30"–40" (75–100 cm). My pipe was about 40" (100 cm) long, which made it a rather tall, slightly swaying lamp.
2. Mount the socket on the threaded pipe and screw in place a generous length of lamp cord. Thread the cord through the still-straight copper pipe and push the bolt down into one end of the pipe.
3. With the cord inserted into the pipe, you can start to shape the pipe into soft curves and bends. Do this carefully, however. If you bend it too tightly, you'll end up getting sharp corners in the pipe. It's better to start by form large curves to begin with, and then tighten them little by little as needed. If you want to be absolutely sure not to get a sharp bend, fill the pipe almost completely full with fine sand and close the opening temporarily with tape. This will hold up the pipe from the inside.

4. A lamp foot made of stone gives the lamp heft and stability. But we want to avoid having to drill into the stone. It's easier to drill into a piece of driftwood, then attach the wood to a stone to make the weight for the base steady. Drill a hole through the wood block for the pipe. Glue the wood block to the stone with super strong construction glue. Let dry.
5. Thread the cord and the pipe through the hole. A few drops of superglue on the pipe where it crosses the wood block give it more stability. It's difficult to glue the rope directly onto shiny metal, so wind some duct tape around each end of the pipe and each side of the wood block to make a surface that the ends of the rope can be glued to. Wind the rope firmly and tightly around the pipe. Attach the rope ends with the glue gun.
6. Tidy up the area around the end of the piping and conceal the lamp socket somewhat with a tassel made from approximately 4" (10 cm) of unraveled and frayed rope. Place the frayed rope around the pipe ends and lash it with the twine.
7. Mount the switch and plug in the cord. Bend the lower end of the pipe so the lamp stand is stabilized against the tabletop.

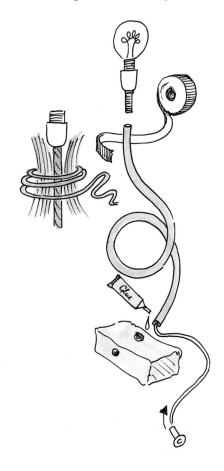

*"BRING HOME A PIECE OF THE BEACH
—A BEAUTIFUL FEATHER, SMOOTH
PEBBLES . . ."*

AN UGLY LAMP FULL OF POTENTIAL. . .

Why spend a fortune in posh home stores when you can scoop up an ugly light fixture at the flea market and turn it into a beautiful decoration for almost nothing? Look at my lamp—this is what it looked like before the makeover began (photo above). The huge shade concealed the fact that the lamp itself looked like a small chandelier. And guess what? This ugly lamp had enough raw materials to make **two** new handsome light fixtures.

A RUSTIC ROPE CHANDELIER

Armed with a bit of patience and a large bundle of rope, you can turn old fashioned lamps or chandeliers to more robust, nautically inspired light fixtures. A few curvy bends covered in rope make the lamp's shape more interesting. However, avoid lamps with too many intricate ornaments. They can be difficult to wrap and cover with rope.

A glue gun is a quick and efficient tool, but it doesn't work on shiny metal. You must prepare the surface where you'll fasten each end of the rope by winding it with textile tape or duct tape, so the rope ends can be glued with the glue gun and attached to the tape. A rope measuring ¼" (6 mm) in diameter has great ropey texture, but on certain parts of the lamp it might be better to use a sturdy natural twine instead. If the lamp has enough surface space to accommodate a thicker rope, ½"–⅝" (12–15 mm) in diameter, it can make a very fine decorative detail (see the midsection of my chandelier). A visible rope joint can be easily hidden by a separate reef knot glued over the joint (see page 117). If you want to take it one step further, you can decorate the chandelier with shells and starfish. Complete the nature of the theme by attaching your decorations with natural twine.

ROPES AND HAWSER ROPE

Nowadays, synthetic ropes and lines are commonly found on boats, but hemp and cotton remain the best options for decorating. Hemp rope, tarred ropes, and hawser rope, 1 ⅜" (36 mm) in diameter, are goods mostly found in maritime supply outlets and ship chandlers in coastal towns.

If you can't find a local supplier, shopping on the Internet is another way to do it. You'll find just about any kind of rope there is at the web shop www.rwrope.com.

SWITCH OUTS

If you start thinking in terms of "I can replace x with rope," then you can come up with completely new and unexpected ways to use rope. Like this rather plain old kitchen chair that first got a new coat of paint and then a whole new look when the wooden strips in the back rest were sawed off and replaced with rope attached with large knots along the chair's back.

WRAPPED AROUND A LAMP BASE

There are plenty of ugly lamp stands in the thrift stores, of which many can be quickly made over with hemp rope into handsome nautical lamps. Try to look past the existing colors and pay particular attention to the design and shape to find a good item for refurbishment.

BEACH FLORA

Take a good look in your storage hideaways. You'll most likely find a few old pots to turn into awesome "new" pots once they have been covered in rope. Even oversized tin cans can be made into hip, modern planters.

Or try something more unusual by winding some rope around a glass vase. Naturally, glass is not the best surface to apply glue to, but rows of rope can be glued to one another. Don't cover the vase entirely—leave some of the glass uncovered at the top as an elegant detail.

An additional variation: Paint plain old ceramic pots with white, matte paint. Wrap a sturdy rope around the pot and make a big knot. Paint both the pot and the rope again. To add more of a beach feel, place the pots on a zinc tray and surround them with beautiful pebbles and shells. Choose simple plants that bring nature and the seashore to mind.

GLUE AND WIND

You can of course cover any surface by winding it with ordinary twine, but it won't impart the same character and beautiful surface texture as rope. Instead, use a thicker hemp or cotton rope. A rope with a diameter of ¼" (6 mm) is pliable and can be used for most things, but if you have a lamp base where a larger-sized rope would work, then by all means use it as the thicker one will look much nicer.

An ordinary glue gun is quick and effective and works on most surfaces except shiny metal; the glue is just not going to stick there. In these cases, textile tape or duct tape can help. You don't have to wind the whole surface with it. Wind only the areas where you start, where you end winding the rope, and where you'll need to attach the rope with glue.

If there's no way to hide the end of the rope, a ¼" (5 mm) diameter rope is thin enough to press down almost flat and then wind over, thereby hiding both ends of the rope.

You can often attach the ends of the rope with a drop of glue and perhaps a staple gun to an area that is hidden from view, such as the underside of a tabletop or under the chair seat. Other times the rope end can be cut into a point and glued down.

You cannot wind from the outside in. The rope must have support where it begins and then builds on itself. A lamp base is wrapped from the top down and then out onto the foot to end at the outer edge. Wind the rope or twine tightly and evenly while you add a spot of glue with the gun at even intervals. A simple reef knot made from two rope ends can be glued on separately as a decorative detail.

ROPE REFINEMENTS

A rope-encased detail can be the difference
between an ordinary and a beachy touch.
Hemp rope in a smaller size, approximately
¼" (6 mm), can be attached and wound
around most things—handles, the backs of
chairs, bed frame legs, and curtain rails.
Just take a look around your home, and
you´ll find all sorts of places that can be
wrapped and covered with rope to make it
look nicer and more nautical. The great
thing here is that you can try it out first and
see how it looks before you decide to make
it permanent and use the glue.

WOODEN BARREL

The ugly ceiling lamp on page 115 became the frame for another light fixture with a maritime feel. You don't need to be a carpenter to switch out the lampshade fabric for some wood and give the lamp a look reminiscent of wood barrels. Really big lampshades are trendy at the moment, so the old lampshade fit perfectly because of its wide frame. And you can find the wooden sticks at the paint store!

MATERIALS:

- Wire frames for lampshade
- Natural twine
- Glue gun
- Sandpaper, medium coarse
- Wood stain/glaze
- Saw
- Flat wood stirring sticks from the paint store are great DIY material! These are flat, thin, and smooth hardwood sticks that come in two sizes. Ask if you can buy a big bundle of them. I have used the bigger ones here.

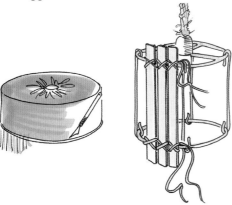

HOW TO:

1. Once I removed the plastic cover on the lampshade, there were only two wide metal wire rings left. The worn metal rings are hidden with wound rope, making them more substantial and sturdy and also providing a good anchor for the glue.

2. Plastic shades typically don't have vertical metal strips connecting the upper and the lower metal ring. To keep the two rings in place while working your new wooden lamp, take four strong metal wires of equal length and bend their ends into hooks. Attach them to the top and bottom metal rings. You can also use a frame that already has the vertical metal support between the upper and lower rings. Mount the cord and lamp socket in the frame right from the start so you can use the cord to hang the frame at a good working height.

3. Cut all the wood sticks to the same length, about 3 ⅛–4" (8–10 cm) longer than the frame's height. Sand the sawn ends smooth with sandpaper. Stain or glaze to your desired color.

4. The wood sticks are attached to the frame with glue from the glue gun. The glue is reinforced by twine wound tightly around both the wood and the metal frame. Tighten with a small knot between the sticks on the interior of the frame. The twine automatically makes a small space between the sticks for the light to shine through. Finish the lampshade off by attaching the ends of the twine.

5. Hide the cord: Hide the unsightly plastic cord by covering a rustic cord with burlap. Cut two long strips from loosely woven burlap, approximately 2" (5 cm) wide and at least twice the cord's length. Pull out a few threads along the long sides of the burlap strips to make them unravel a bit. Put the strips together and sew a zigzag seam along both long sides. Feed the cord through the channel between the two seams.

THE CAPTAIN'S COMPASS CARD

A mariner's compass card has a strict design with straight lines, sharp points and angles, which makes it a very edgy and distinct decorative item. It's exactly what I needed to breathe some life into a few pieces of older, unremarkable thrift-store furniture, and to decorate a cozy corner with some nautical highlights in the summer cottage—the captain's own lounge.

A COMPASS CUSHION

A handsome, well-made cushion with a compass card sewn on in appliqué is a perfect fit for a captain's lounge. The compass card has a slightly more rounded shape to allow you to cut out all pieces from fabric. They're attached with close zigzag stitching, so the seams make an attractive edging on the motif, too.

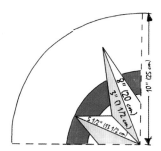

MATERIALS:

You'll need batting or fiberfill for pillows. The cushion cover itself is made of sturdy cotton or linen. Use more lightweight cotton fabric for appliqués if you prefer. Vliesofix, a fusible web for appliqué, will make the appliqué stick (see page 56).

HOW TO:

1. Draw a whole circle pattern following the diagram. Make paper patterns for a circle measuring 1 ⅝" (4 cm) in diameter and for the different light and dark halves of the points in the compass card. You can even draw up the pattern directly on the paperbacked fusible web. Iron the fusible web on the wrong side of the appliquéd fabric. Cut out all pieces for the compass card.

2. Center the round red circle on the round piece of fabric. Attach it by ironing the fabric with a warm iron. Set the sewing machine to make a close zigzag seam, stitch length set to 0.8 - 1 and width 4. Sew a zigzag seam along the circle's inner and outer edges.

3. Use the iron again and attach all the small pieces for the compass card. When they're all in place, stitch them on with a close zigzag seam along the outside edge.

4. If adding letters, paint them on using stencils (see page 142).

5. Fold the paper pattern for the cushion cover in half and add a ¾" (2 cm) seam allowance along the straight side. Cut two back pieces for the cushion. Stitch together the pieces along the straight side, but leave about a 8" (20 cm) opening in the seam.

6. Place front and back pieces together, right side against right side. Stitch the cushion using a ⅝" (1 ½ cm) seam allowance all around. Cut V-shaped notches out of the seam allowance evenly spaced all around the cushion. Turn the cushion inside out. Press. Sew a decorative topstitch all around the cushion about ¾" (2 cm) in from the outer edge.

7. Use the same pattern to sew an inner case from the sheeting fabric. Fill the case with batting or fiberfill. Pull the cushion cover over the inner case and sew the seam opening together by hand.

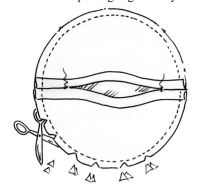

121

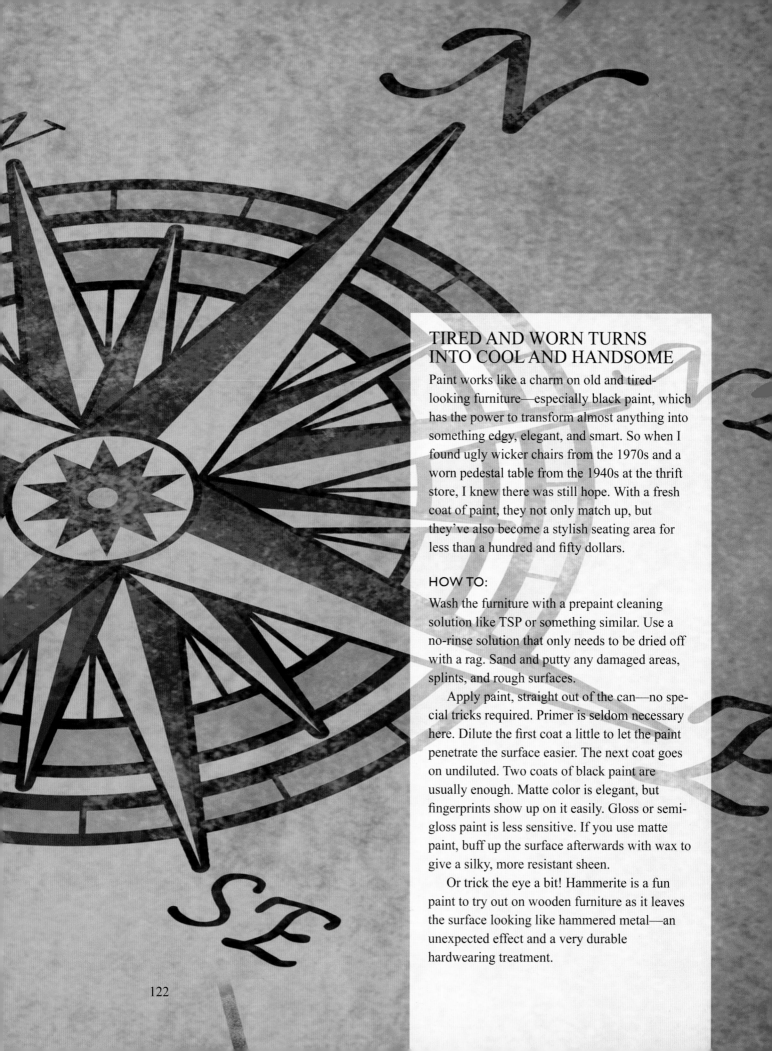

TIRED AND WORN TURNS INTO COOL AND HANDSOME

Paint works like a charm on old and tired-looking furniture—especially black paint, which has the power to transform almost anything into something edgy, elegant, and smart. So when I found ugly wicker chairs from the 1970s and a worn pedestal table from the 1940s at the thrift store, I knew there was still hope. With a fresh coat of paint, they not only match up, but they've also become a stylish seating area for less than a hundred and fifty dollars.

HOW TO:

Wash the furniture with a prepaint cleaning solution like TSP or something similar. Use a no-rinse solution that only needs to be dried off with a rag. Sand and putty any damaged areas, splints, and rough surfaces.

Apply paint, straight out of the can—no special tricks required. Primer is seldom necessary here. Dilute the first coat a little to let the paint penetrate the surface easier. The next coat goes on undiluted. Two coats of black paint are usually enough. Matte color is elegant, but fingerprints show up on it easily. Gloss or semi-gloss paint is less sensitive. If you use matte paint, buff up the surface afterwards with wax to give a silky, more resistant sheen.

Or trick the eye a bit! Hammerite is a fun paint to try out on wooden furniture as it leaves the surface looking like hammered metal—an unexpected effect and a very durable hardwearing treatment.

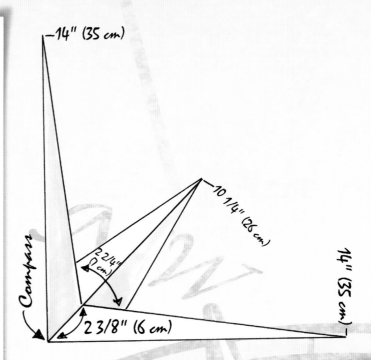

14" (35 cm)

Compass

10 1/4" (26 cm)

14" (35 cm)

2 2/4" (7 cm)

2 3/8" (6 cm)

Arrow

LONGITUDE AND LATITUDE

Whip up some new slipcovers and cushions for the wicker chair. The most affordable way to get foam rubber for the cushions is by purchasing foam rubber mattresses with a depth of 2" to 2 ¾" (5–7 cm) from a discount store. Draw the shape of the cushion directly onto the foam rubber with a black marker. Cut the foam with a pair of scissors or carpet knife if the foam is a bit thicker. Wrap the foam in a piece of batting to soften the edges of the cushion. Then wrap it in cotton sheeting, just as if you were wrapping up a parcel. Baste the cotton wrap together by hand. The cushion is now ready to be covered with the slipcover fabric.

The slipcover pattern is the same as for the foam cushion, except now you have to add a seam allowance. I know you've added the puffy batting, which enlarges the original foam cushion, but the slipcover needs to be tight-fitting over the padded cushion to make it retain its shape.

The covers for the captain's chairs are made of sturdy old linen towels, patched and mended with different white and natural fabrics. The lettering is stenciled. That way, if the covers get a stain or two that cannot be removed in the laundry, you can just cover the stain by stitching on another patch or a stencil in another letter.

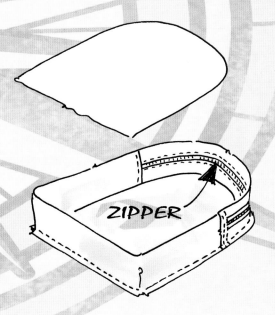

ZIPPER

A CIRCLE

Many a veneered coffee table is truly beautiful, but we don't notice it for the all-empowering brown wood. They're often drab looking, worn, and scratched with a damaged finish. With a bit of TLC and patient sanding, however, the table-top will get its looks back—all it takes is some patience working with the machine sander and painting the rest of the table in another color to enhance the tabletop further. Dramatic, drawn-out points of a compass card are painted directly onto the wooden surface, and the different shades of veneer became integral to the illustration of the compass.

TABLE TOP:

1. Sand, sand, and sand some more. You'll need a bit of patience to get the veneer clean with some medium-grain sandpaper. All old varnish needs to be removed so the surface is clean and matte.
2. Using the diagram, draw a compass card on the tabletop with a pencil. Apply masking tape along the outer edges of the compass card. Rub the tape on. Paint the whole compass card in white with ordinary white primer. It'll take at least two coats, maybe a few more, before the white covers the surface entirely.
3. Once the white paint has had a chance to dry completely and has (preferably) rested an extra day to cure, tape the contour for the black fields. Rub the tape on completely. Paint with black, water-based, acrylic paint. You might need to apply two coats. Remove the tape carefully while the paint is still wet.
4. Letters for the four cardinal points and the small triangular arrow are stenciled on. (Read about stenciling on page 142.)
5. Once the paint is completely dry, sand it lightly with fine-grain sandpaper. Do not want to wear off the whole compass card, just make the paint more matte so it will look "softer" and a bit used. Protect the decorative paint by treating the wood's surface with wax.

"PERHAPS WE HAVE INHERITED, FROM TIMES IMMEMORIAL, A GENE THAT INSTINCTIVELY PULLS US TO WATER BECAUSE WATER EQUATES TO SURVIVAL."

CHRISTMAS AT BLACK MALIN'S

A life at the beach! Does this conjure up images of summer, sun, glimmering water, and softly bobbing boats? It would be a lot of work to change this decor around completely once fall arrives . . . so no. It goes without saying that your seafront and maritime decor works just as well in cold weather as it does during the summertime. After all, your love of the sea and the ocean hasn't ebbed simply because a winter chill has set in. Red, white, stripes, star patterns, natural linen, hemp rope, and natural twine—hear, hear . . . Christmas and the nautical style do have much in common, so they make a well-matched pair! Come with me to visit my dear sister, Black Malin, a sea captain with the license to sail all seven seas, and get some nautical Christmas inspiration!

BLACK MALIN'S CHRISTMAS TREE. . .

. . . is—naturally—festooned with the sea captain's favorites. Some are homemade; others are bought and then given a makeover to suit.

- A garland of flags is, of course, made up of signal flags! They don't have to be exact copies. Any fabrics in colors and patterns that remind you of signal flags will be good enough mimics to carry the message. Cut the fabric into pieces measuring 1 ½" x 4" (4 cm x 10 cm). Brush them with glue (Mod Podge, wood glue, hobby glue, or tapestry glue—they all work fine) and fold them in half around some twine. Once dry, they'll be stiff and easy to shape with scissors. Cut some of them to a sharp point.

- Small, small wooden boats can often be found in gift and souvenir shops. Dress them up for the Holidays by brushing on some PVA glue and sprinkle them with glitter.

- Tubes of silvery glitter glue were used to spruce up the store-bought black ball ornaments with pirate skulls.

- A bit more work is required for the mini lifesavers. Paint old wooden curtain rings in red and white. Glitter-glue from a tube is brushed on top of the paint. The "rope" on the lifesaver is made from a piece of string taped on with small strips of silvery duct tape.

- Small anchors are cut out of thin metal or card stock. Soak the metal in some apple cider vinegar for one hour, and it will start to rust once it's removed. A bit of fine salt will speed the process along. Both metal and paper can be brushed with glitter glue in gold or bronze/brown colors.

129

MAPS ON THE GIFT PARCELS

Sea charts and maps become handsome Christmas wrapping paper tied with rope, hemp string, and tarred string (for its smell). You can give all papers—sea charts, ordinary maps—a nice patina finish and an old fashioned, yellow, aged look by merely brushing on some regular coffee. If you only have a limited amount of maps or sea charts, use them sparingly by adding them as decorative strips around parcels first wrapped in plain paper. The smaller pieces and scraps can step in as gift labels.

KRAFT PAPER PARCELS

Soft parcels? Well, almost! Ordinary brown paper, when first balled together very tightly and then pressed flat, starts to feel a bit fluffy and soft and makes a nice wrapping paper. You can highlight the wrinkles by gently brushing the paper by hand with some paint. Use white paint for a natural look or go for silver or gold for a fun clash of metal gloss on brown wrapping paper. Tie the parcel with natural colored ribbon or twine and decorate with glued-on sea and mussel shells. Make the seashells even more festive by brushing them with some glitter glue.

SANTA'S GIFT BAG IS A SEAMAN'S BUCKET!

Sewn from coarse linen or burlap and stenciled with red lettering, a "Seaman's bucket" becomes a handsome receptacle for storing Christmas gifts. Or leave out the text, and it can be used year-round. (You'll find the instructions on how to make the Seaman's bucket on page 74.)

PIRATE, FOR SURE!

Graceful and coarse, elegant and pirate rough!
Style collisions and contrasts can be a lot of fun.
An overly ornate dining chair from a nineteenth-
century salon becomes a handsome pirate chair
when the seat is decorated with a pirate skull.
Where can you find such fabric? You'll paint it
yourself, naturally! (Check out pages 142–143.)

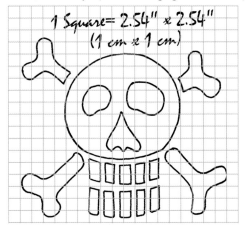

1, 2, 3, 4 SUNDAYS IN ADVENT

Little pirates tend to keep a close eye on the Advent
calendar. Old-timey clothes pegs, acrylic paint from
the craft store, a small fine brush, and a steady hand
are all that's needed. Brown paper bags can be
purchased or made out of strong Kraft paper, which is
machine-sewn along the sides.

A SHIP ARRIVES LOADED

Four holes with enough space for candles are the most
important criteria on an Advent candleholder. With
those in place, even an old, rough board from the beach
can become Christmas-worthy—perhaps left with its
attractive patina or with some added wooden blocks to
turn it into a cargo ship. Use ordinary acrylic paint
from the craft store on the wood, but dilute it with a lot
of water to make it more like a glaze, which will still
leave the texture and feel of the wood underneath. Drill
holes measuring $\frac{7}{8}$" (22 mm) in diameter and spaced
approximately 3 $\frac{1}{2}$" to 4" (9 cm–10 cm) apart. Place
metal candleholder inserts (from the craft store) inside
the drilled holes.

AMBIENCE IN THE SAND

Chase the winter gloom away with plenty of light! Fill
a large platter with fine sand, and you'll have a
"candleholder" that accommodates all types of
candles—simply wedge them in the sand. They'll stay
secured and burn safely all the way down to the
bottom. When they reach the sand, they'll extinguish
themselves. If you have large shells (you might be able
to find them at thrift stores, since it was once popular
to serve seafood in them), you can stick them in the
sand, two by two, and insert a candle in between—a
quick, beach-themed variation on a lantern.

PEARL MUSSELS

Are you having mussels for dinner? Then save their
shells and boil them in ordinary water to sanitize
them. Brush them with glue and dust them in color-
less glitter—they'll soon be beautifully shimmery
inside. Fasten a pearl to the inside of each shell. A
wreath frame can be made of straw or styrolite. Tear
thin strips of black fabric and wind them around the
frame. Use a glue gun to secure the mussels close to
each other until the whole wreath is covered in shells.

then needs to be looped three times (instead of two) to hide the plywood support. First, securely fasten the rope with electrician's tape, masking tape, or textile tape. Then cut through the rope using a sharp saw with fine teeth. Hawser—one piece 35 ¼" (88 cm) + one piece 44" (110 cm). Each piece is coiled in a circle to make the ends meet. Adjust the pieces as needed. Glue the ends together with a glue gun. Then glue the hawser/rope onto the support.

3. Rope used to wind around the hawser coils is thinner, measuring about ¼"–⁵⁄₁₆" (6 mm–8 mm). Try to wind six rows around the wreath to calculate how much rope you'll need. Cut four such identical lengths of this rope. In a large glass jar, mix red acrylic paint with a lot of water to make a watery glaze. Place the rope in the red water and let it soak up the color for a few hours. Hang it up to dry.

4. The small rope end at the bottom of the hawser wreath is a loose, separate piece of rope with a knot in each end. Secure the rope's end against the wreath with your glue gun. Wind the red rope tightly around the wreath. Attach the rope ends to the back of the wreath with the glue gun. Decorate the wreath by hanging a pendant in the middle hole. I was fortunate enough to find a star made out of sheet metal. Similar stars can be found at a local craft store or in any Christmas section at your local department store.

SKIPPER'S WREATH

A thick, sturdy, hawser rope breathes the air of the ocean and its salty waves, so the best nautical Christmas wreath must be this one made from hawser rope that's wound with red-colored hemp rope.

HOW TO:

1. The wreaths must be mounted against a flat support. If you can, saw the supports out of thin plywood. Otherwise cut out some thick cardboard with an X-acto blade or other sharp knife. Make the support circle round, 14" (35 cm) in diameter and 2 ½" (6 cm) wide. Make two small holes in the support, fasten some steel wire through them, and make a loop to hang the wreath.

2. Two rows of hawser rope, 1 ½" (36 mm) in diameter, look fantastic. If you can't find it in a local store, purchase it in the web shop www.rwrope.com. A less costly alternative, however, is a slightly narrower hemp rope measuring 1" (25 mm) diameter, which

SAY IT WITH A ROPE

Hand lettering with rope? Of course you can. Your family name, perhaps the name of your house or farm, or any word that is special to you . . . CHRISTMAS written out in rope is definitely a nautically inspired Christmas decoration.

Use a piece of rope measuring ½"–¾" (12 mm–18 mm) in diameter. Estimate the length of rope you'll need by first laying it out in your handwriting. Place the rope in a can of wallpaper paste and let it soak for a few days so the rope absorbs the glue. Remove the rope from the tin and remove any excess glue. "Write" your chosen word with the rope on a flat surface protected by plastic. It will take quite a while for the glue to dry completely, so once you've finished writing you'll need to leave the rope alone for a week. When the glue is dry, the rope will be stiff. Wind the letters in some places with natural twine to give it better shape and firmness. Suspend the writing with small tacks or twine as seen in the picture.

Plumbi acetas

GENTLEMAN
Mixture
N.º 508
SMOKING TOBACCO

Jul is Swedish for Christmas.

WOODLAND MARKERS

Green is also a maritime color, even if it's not as commonly encountered in other nautically inspired interiors or decorations. Many sea markers are green, which is where we got inspiration for these nifty, pointy fir trees.

MATERIALS:

- Small, wooden paint stirring sticks, approximately ⅝" (15 mm) wide, from the paint store
- A stick or tree branch from the woods, measuring 11"–14" (30 cm–35 cm) long and ½"–⅝" (12 mm–15 mm) in diameter
- A piece of flat wood, approximately 4" x 4" (10 cm x 10 cm)
- Glue
- Small screws, approximately ½" (13 mm) long
- Green acrylic paint

TOOLS

- Fine saw
- Drill bit, ½" (12 mm) diameter
- Power drill
- Sandpaper, medium grain
- Screwdriver
- Paint brush

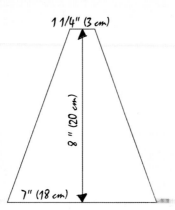

1 1/4" (3 cm)

8 " (20 cm)

7" (18 cm)

HOW TO:

1. Place nine to thirteen wooden, paint-stirring sticks close together on a flat surface. Draw the fir tree's outline. Cut the sticks with your saw and sand the sawed-off short ends with the medium grain sandpaper. Sand the flat piece of wood, too.
2. Dilute the paint with water until it becomes a glaze and paint both sticks and the flat wood piece green.
3. The stick or tree branch is the tree's trunk. Neaten it with a whittling knife and make the stick narrower at the bottom if needed. Glue it onto the flat, wooden piece. Glue all the painted sticks onto the trunk. Start at the top and work your way downward while turning each second stick 90°. While the glue gun makes fast work of this, the glue can easily lose its grip. Drill a small hole in each stick and reinforce the glue by adding a small screw. This extra step will make these fir tree decorations last much longer.

GLAMMED UP BUOY

Red glitter and shiny metallic silver matched up with robust hemp rope equals a winning and glamorous clash of styles. For a Christmas-ready front door, attach a branch of winter evergreen decorated with coils of rope and a festive, shimmering buoy.

SMALL LIFE BUOYS

A sleek look, that is so charming and simple to make. Put several together in one go because you're sure to find other ways to decorate with these.

MATERIALS:

- Wreath frame made of styrolite 6"–8" (15–20 cm) in diameter
- White cotton fabric
- Wood glue for outside use
- White and red acrylic paint
- Red glitter glue
- Silver duct tape
- Hemp rope, 25 ½" (65 cm) long, ¼" (6 mm) in diameter

HOW TO:

1. Cut strips on the bias, approximately ¾" (2 cm) wide, out of the cotton fabric. Wind the strips tightly around the styrolite wreath frame until they cover it completely. The wood glue, which can be rather gummy, should be diluted with some water and then brushed over the whole wreath. Once the glue has dried, the wreath will have a fabric-covered surface, which is far more durable and attractive than just the styrolite.

2. Paint two opposing quarters of the wreath in white and the other quarters in red. Let dry. Paint red glitter glue over the red painted surfaces.

3. Pull out and loosely attach some duct tape to a mirrored surface. Cut the tape down the middle with an X-acto blade or other sharp knife to make the strips half as wide. With the strips of duct tape, fasten the rope against the wreath over the borderlines of the red and white painted areas.

ABUNDANT CHRISTMAS SPLENDOR

A lot of Christmas for the money! Here, small Christmas boats surf across waves of winter green! The simpler or more minimalistic your interior decorating, the more effective it'll be to decorate your surroundings with festively abundant garlands. This one is simple to put together yourself.

HOW TO:

1. A coarse hemp hawser, 1 ½" (36 mm) in diameter, is the star of this show. Start by trying out the length you'll need. Make two long loops out of slightly thinner rope for hanging the garland, and attach the loops with some glue to the back of each end of the hemp hawser. To reinforce the glue, wind about an inch (a few centimeters) of twine tightly around each end.

2. To be practical, let's choose some straggly looking–but artificial—greenery; it's durable and remains green. A completely natural option is to use a few bare birch branches instead. Attach just a few branches together with thin metal wire. It's meant to look airy and a bit sparse.

3. Lay the thinner rope in large, loose loops, as in a figure eight, and secure it against the garland's middle. Glue a life buoy straight across the rope coils.

4. Small, Christmassy sailboats are made of driftwood with a wooden skewer used as a mast. The fabric for the sail is brushed with glue (Mod Podge, wood glue, wallpaper paste, etc.) and left to dry. Once it's dry and the fabric is stiff, paint a small star on the sail and make a small hole in the sail to place it on the mast. It'll stay on the mast

by itself. Brush glue on a strip of fabric and fold it in half across the mast's top. Once the glue is dry, the fabric will be stiff and can be cut into a pointy pennant. Drill a small hole in the driftwood hull. Pull a thin metal wire through it so you can fasten it onto the hawser rope.

DRIFTWOOD STICKS

The small fir tree made from random treasures found on the beach is a serene beauty. Paint an old board in a color that will blend into the background (the same color as the wall where you want to hang or stand the fir tree). Then simply glue pieces of driftwood onto the board in order of size. A small decorative star caps it and transforms your collection of wood sticks into a Christmas tree. If you don't have a starfish, use an ordinary star in some other material.

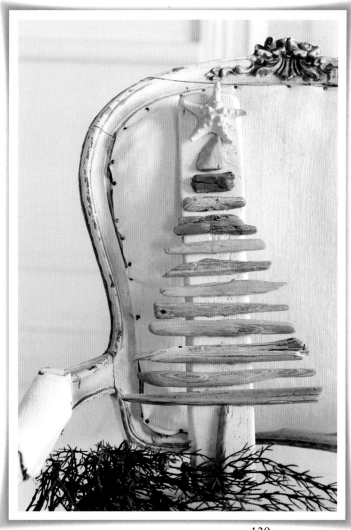

STENCILING
& STAMPING

MATERIALS:

- Textile paint, or acrylic paint meant for different surfaces and wood
- Paper plate
- Masking tape
- Dense foam rubber + rubber band + wooden stick
- Stencils or stamps, found at craft stores
- Metal stencils in shape of letters and numbers, found at interior decorating stores selling country or cottage style items
- Rubber-like stamps for letters and numbers, found in hobby stores

HOW TO PAINT:

1. Yes, you could buy stenciling brushes or dense foam rollers. But the cheapest and just as sufficient tool is your own sponge brush made of dense foam rubber. Cut a strip, 1 ½" x 1 ½" x 10", fold it around a wooden stick (or a pencil), and hold together with a rubber band. Pour out a small amount of paint on a paper plate.

2. Stencil: Attach the stencil to your desired surface with masking tape. Press the foam brush into the paint. First try out stamping on a piece of scratch paper to make sure big blotches of paint aren't right on top of the foam's surface. That would just smudge. By stamping a few times on a spare paper, the foam will soak up the paint. Then stamp lightly over the stencil. Better to stamp on several thin layers of paint than to be impatient and try to get coverage the first time, which will just give you a messy result. You don´t have to strive for full coverage—leave it a bit uneven and light in different spots.

3. Stamp: If you have a rubber stamp instead of a stencil, you can use acrylic paint or textile paint on that, too. Normally, the stamp is pressed on an ink-soaked pad. Use the foam to transfer paint to the stamp. Then press the stamp, color-side down, against the fabric or wood. Be careful not to move the stamp sideways and rub and smudge the surface. Lift the stamp straight up from the surface.

MAKE YOUR OWN STENCILS

You can make your own stencils with motifs and letters—all kinds of letter fonts can be found on the computer. But did you know that you can print them as big as you want? The size of the paper is your only limit.

In the MS Word program, go to the font selection's sizing window. There are many preselected sizes, but if you select the window you can type your own custom size with the number keys. Try this: select size 200, and then type something. Oops, there you are! It works up to 999, but it likely won't fit on your chosen paper.

This allows you to type letters in whatever size or style you want. Most fonts/styles of lettering are not made for stenciling, of course. If you try to cut out the letters, the paper and the empty spaces will not stay in one piece. To make it work as a stencil, make small "bridges" so the letters are divided in smaller sections. Below is an example with the font "Georgia" in bold:

SJÖ

becomes

SJÖ

HOW TO:

1. Whether you make stencils out of letters or decorative motifs, draw them on ordinary paper first. Then attach clear, self-adhesive plastic on both sides of the paper. Cut out the pattern in the plastic with an X-acto knife or another sharp knife. Having a glass surface underneath makes this task much easier!

2. The stencil's wrong side can be sprayed with a stencil spray adhesive from the craft or paint store. This makes the stencil stick flat on top of the surface to be painted, but still easy to remove when you're done painting.

PAINT STRIPES

Painting stripes onto fabric is not difficult. Stripes can be taped directly onto the fabric with masking tape. Paint the fabric with textile paint. Use a piece of dense foam rubber, dip it in paint, and then press it against the fabric. Let it dry. Textile colors need to be set with an iron before they can be run through the laundry.

FABRICS

All fabrics that will be laundered after being painted will also need to be laundered prior to being painted. Use textile paint that is set by ironing the fabric. Acrylic paint for craft or furniture will work just fine if you're not planning to wash the fabric (as would be the case with a lampshade, for example). The fabric to be painted is placed onto a flat surface covered with a protective paper in case the paint bleeds through.

The spaces for the skull's eye sockets and nose are separate details and are not part of the big stencil. If you're using stencil spray adhesive, you can cut out those pieces and attach them directly to the fabric. However, if you're painting a white skull, you might find it easier to paint the basic white shape first, and then with a brush, paint the eyes and nose on top of the white skull.

*". . . BRING THAT BEACHFRONT
FEELING HOME TO SATISFY
THE YEARNING IN YOUR
HEART . . ."*